BIG BOOK of BIBLE STORY ART ACTIVITIES

Gospel Light

HOW TO MAKE CLEAN COPIES FROM THIS BOOK

You may make copies of portions of this book with a clean conscience if

☀ you (or someone in your organization) are the original purchaser;

☀ you are using the copies you make for a noncommercial purpose (such as teaching or promoting your ministry) within your church or organization;

☀ you follow the instructions provided in this book.

However, it is ILLEGAL for you to make copies if

☀ you are using the material to promote, advertise or sell a product or service other than for ministry fund-raising;

☀ you are using the material in or on a product for sale; or

☀ you or your organization are not the original purchaser of this book.

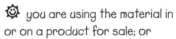

Gospel Light

Editorial Staff

Founder, Dr. Henrietta Mears

Publisher Emeritus, William T. Greig

Publisher, Children's Curriculum and Resources, Lynnette Pennings, M.A.

Senior Consulting Publisher, Dr. Elmer L. Towns

Managing Editor, Sheryl Haystead

Senior Consulting Editor, Wesley Haystead, M.S.Ed.

Senior Editor, Biblical and Theological Issues, Bayard Taylor, M.Div.

Editorial Team, Debbie Barber, Rebecca Garcia, Karen McGraw

Art Directors, Lenndy McCullough, Christina Renée Sharp, Samantha A. Hsu

Designer, Zelle Olson

How to Use This Book

This book offers 100 art activities and Bible stories that you can use for fun and interactive Bible learning with young children. Each art activity provides clear easy-to-follow instructions along with several enrichment ideas and suggestions for guided conversation. Each Bible story is written with age-appropriate vocabulary for use with young children.

If You Are a Teacher

1. Use the contents page and/or index to locate activities that coordinate with the Bible stories you are teaching. Plan to use the activities as an alternative to or enrichment of your curriculum.

2. To prepare each activity, collect the materials needed. Read the Bible story on the back of the activity page and familiarize yourself with the suggestions for guided conversation provided in the Talk About section of the activity. (See "Connecting the Bible to Life" on p. 7 for tips on talking with young children about Bible truths.)

3. Tell and talk about the Bible story in one or more ways:

☀ Tell the story before children complete the art activity.

☀ Talk about the story while children work on the art activity.

☀ Invite children to take turns telling the story, using their completed art projects to illustrate story events.

If You Are the Director or Coordinator

The activities and Bible stories from *The Big Book of Bible Story Art Activities for Ages 3 to 6* can be used to supplement your regular teaching program. Use the contents page and/or index to locate activities that coordinate with the Bible stories taught in the curriculum you are using. Photocopy the activity and Bible story to give to teachers to use in lessons as an alternative to or enrichment of the curriculum.

You may also use the pages as the foundation for Sunday evening or weekday early childhood programs, Mother's Morning Out or any other time programming is needed for children ages three to six. Photocopy the activity and Bible story for each teacher and helper. After hearing the Bible story, children complete the art activity. Add a snack and/or playtime as needed to fill the time.

Basic Art Materials

The materials for each activity are listed with each activity. However, collecting materials will be easy if you have plenty of the following supplies on hand: newspaper or plastic tablecloths (to protect surfaces), scissors, glue bottles and glue sticks, markers, crayons, chalk, tape, play dough, discarded magazines and catalogs, collage materials (yarn, ribbon, cotton balls, chenille wire, etc.), colored and white construction paper, stapler and staples, paint smocks (men's old short-sleeved shirts from a thrift shop serve well) and butcher paper.

Contents

Teacher Enrichment Articles

Bible Story Art Activities

Bible Story Character Index

Connecting the Bible to Life

Why do we need to guide conversation with young children? Don't we simply talk to them? Certainly there are many times when simple conversation is spontaneous. However, guided conversation helps children remember and recognize ways to apply the Bible truth that is the foundation for the art activity.

What is guided conversation? Does it mean the teacher spends every minute spouting story facts? Talking only when a problem arises? No! Guided conversation is simply informal but planned conversation in which the teacher looks for opportunities to connect the Bible story to what children are doing. Relating the children's activities to Bible truths helps each child understand the relationship between what he or she is doing and what the Bible says.

Step One: Be familiar with the Bible story and the life-focus statement provided for each art activity. This prepares you to share these ideas whenever natural opportunities and teachable moments occur.

Step Two: Listen. The biggest part of being a skilled teacher is being a good listener. When children are absorbed in an activity, don't take a break or leave the area. Place yourself at the children's eye level, available to hear. Listening and observing provide you with helpful insight into each child's thoughts and feelings. Watch and listen for clues to their interests, how they see themselves and what things might bother them. Resist the temptation to tune a child out or mentally race ahead.

Step Three: Ask questions. Invite children into conversation that involves more than answering yes or no. Ask open-ended questions that invite the child to describe and discuss! Use the comments and questions provided in the Talk About section of each activity. Questions and comments that cannot be answered with a yes or no help children learn verbal skills, help them express their feelings and give you greater insight into their thoughts and feelings.

Step Four: Relate the child's thoughts and feelings to God's Word! You might begin by commenting on what you see. "Sheena, you helped Jake! God tells us to help each other. Thank you!" You may also rephrase a child's words. "It sounds like you had a happy time with Delia, Mike. Our Bible story tells us about two friends. God gives us friends. We can thank God for Delia. Thank You, God, for Mike's friend Delia!"

When you identify acts of kindness or helpfulness, children then learn what it means to help

each other, share or take turns. Relate a child's actions immediately, before children forget the circumstances. And use the child's name. Often, a child who does not hear his or her name assumes you are talking to someone else!

As you see children experience satisfaction, curiosity or even frustration, you are witnessing teachable moments. Children are especially receptive to new ideas at such times. Step in with a comment or question that will help the child resolve the problem; affirm a child's accomplishment with an "I see . . ." comment; answer a child's question and thank God for the child's curiosity on the spot!

With the session's Bible truths in mind, you are ready to listen, observe and comment in ways that will help each child understand more about how God's love and God's Word relate to his or her world.

Note
This article, revised for use in this book, originally appeared in *Early Childhood Smart Pages* (Ventura, CA: Gospel Light, 2002), pp. 9-10.

Creative Art for Young Children

Art activities are among the most used—and most misunderstood—experiences offered to young children. Young children have no sense whatsoever of what adults expect them to produce when art materials are offered. They are small scientists: for them, art materials are not a means to make a pretty product by adult standards but the means to discover what happens when, for instance, random paper scraps are stacked together and glued into a pile!

Process, Not Product

For young children, using art materials is about the experience of creating and the process of discovering. Remember that for young children it is the process, not the product, that matters. Encourage children to explore materials freely. Relax and recognize that sometimes it is a greater learning experience to swirl the glue with fingers than it is to create what the teacher had in mind! Art gives children the chance to express their feelings and thoughts and to release tension as well. Give them freedom to experiment creatively.

Helping, Not Hindering

As a child and teacher use art materials together in a relaxed and creative way, natural

opportunities arise for conversation. Such teachable moments often provide the perfect times to help a child understand vital Bible truths! "I see lots of blue in your picture, James. What other things did God make that are blue?" "God gave you hands that can draw lots of little circles, Josie. Let's thank Him!" Include God in your conversation through word, prayer or song to positively reinforce how much God values that child!

When a child shows you his or her work, invite the child into conversation about the art. NEVER ask, "What is it?" The comment to make is, "Emily, tell me about your picture!" or "I see many squiggly lines, Kyle—tell me about those lines." And NEVER attempt to fix or finish what you think needs to be changed in any child's art.

If a child says, "Draw it for me," suggest, "Let's see how much you can do by yourself first." Encourage the child and help him or her feel assured that no one will judge his or her work.

A child may comment, "Leo's picture is ugly!" or "He copied me. That's not fair!" Deal gently with both the critic and the criticized. "Mason, Leo made his picture the way he wanted it." You may also say, "If Leo's picture is like your picture, that's OK. Leo must have really liked your picture." Don't put down the child who voiced the criticism; instead, help the child see that each person's work is valued.

Preparation

For children to enjoy an art project, they need to hear as few warnings as possible. They need to feel successful. As you get to know the personalities and capabilities of each child, you can tailor the activity to the group's needs. And a little preparation will go a long way in keeping a small mess from becoming a big one!

Cover tabletops and floors with newspaper or plastic tablecloths. Secure on all sides with masking tape.

Keep a supply of premoistened towelettes, no-rinse hand-wiping solution or paper towels handy for messy fingers and small spills. Set a trash can where children can clean up easily.

Activities that use potentially messy materials (glue, paint, etc.) may be difficult if your teacher/child ratio is too large or if you do not have adequate space or furniture. In such cases, you may need to substitute easier materials (crayons, etc.) for the activity.

Note
This article, revised for use in this book, originally appeared in *Early Childhood Smart Pages* (Ventura, CA: Gospel Light, 2002), pp. 87–88.

Getting Children's Attention

When it's time to give directions or get children's attention, children may be told, "Sit still until everyone is here" or "Wait in line until we are ready." Such methods of gaining attention and control are self-defeating if we are trying to teach kindness and respect through our own behavior. They also create negative feelings and waste valuable teaching time. There are better ways!

When You Want to Start

It's easy to establish a simple attention-getting signal for the children in your group. Choose a signal to use and introduce the signal with spoken directions. It's a good idea to practice using the signal until the children are familiar with it. Once children know the routine, simply give the signal and allow children time to respond. Always acknowledge the children who respond quickly to the signal and thank each child by name. Here are a few signal ideas:

☺ Flick lights on and off two or three times.

☺ Slowly count aloud to five to see if everyone can be quietly looking at you before you say "five."

☺ Hold up two fingers (or hold up a different number of fingers each time) and invite children whose attention you've gained to tell how many fingers you are holding up.

☺ Sing the same song or play the same music before the same activity at each session. "By the time the song is finished, you should all be sitting on the floor."

☺ Ring a bell. (Collect several different bells. Make a game of identifying which bell you rang.)

☺ Clap hands in a pattern. Children imitate pattern as you gain their attention.

☺ Say "One, two, three—all eyes on me." (Follow this with a question: "What color is my sweater?" or "What animal do you think is on the back of my shirt?")

☺ Use a finger-play poem or other chant for children to imitate. (Change finger plays to keep interest high, but do the same one consistently for a while, so children know that finger play is a signal.)

☺ As children gather, sing a song that includes each of their names. Others will hurry to join you to hear their names sung!

While Children Listen

There are times in any activity or story time when some children lose interest. Plan ahead for these times! To regain a child's attention, try these ideas:

☼ Ask a question, using a child's name.

☼ Whisper your words, which often generates renewed interest from children.

☼ Change the pace by leading children in a finger play, an action song or a simple imitation game to recall attention.

Always phrase directions to even the most wiggly child in terms of what he or she can do instead of what not to do. "Ryan, you need to glue the pictures onto the paper. I'm looking to see what pictures you are going to choose!"

How to Get Your Message Across

Here are some tips for effective communication with young children:

☼ Get the child's attention before speaking. Adults waste lots of breath saying things when no one is listening. For example, shouting across a room to a child results in confusion rather than communication. Go to the child. Bend down so that your face is at his or her eye level. Speak the child's name. "Seth, it's time for you to put the markers in the can."

☼ Say the most important words first. After you've spoken the child's name, briefly state what you want the child to do. Then you may add a reason. "Karla, put your paper by the door. It's almost time for your dad to come."

☼ Use simple words and a natural tone of voice. Speak slowly and distinctly in a soft yet audible tone. Let your voice express your enthusiasm and interest. Add a smile to your words. Avoid baby talk or gushing.

☼ Use specific words. General terms leave a child confused, not knowing exactly what you mean. Rather than "Put the toys away," say, "Alex, your red truck needs to go here on this shelf."

Note
This article, revised for use in this book, originally appeared in *Early Childhood Smart Pages* (Ventura, CA: Gospel Light, 2002), pp. 125-126.

Sun and Moon Mosaics

Collect

Bible, construction paper (yellow, white, black and light blue), two plastic bowls, white and yellow crayons and/or chalk, glue.

Prepare

Tear yellow and white construction paper into small scraps for mosaic pieces. Place each color in a different bowl. (Note: For large classes, prepare a set of bowls for each group of four to six children.)

Do

1. Children use white crayons or chalk to draw moons on sheets of black construction paper and yellow crayons or chalk to draw suns on sheets of blue construction paper.

2. Children fill drawn moon outlines by gluing mosaic pieces of white construction paper within the outlines. Children fill drawn sun outlines by gluing mosaic pieces of yellow construction paper within the outlines.

Enrichment Ideas

1. Older children tear paper to make mosaic pieces. Children glue cotton balls for clouds on sun pictures and place star stickers on moon pictures.

2. Provide gel pens for children to use in drawing on black paper.

3. Children brush thinned glue over sun outline and then place yellow tissue-paper scraps on outline.

God Made the World

Genesis 1:1-19

I'm thankful God made the world.

Talk About

☼ In today's Bible story, God made the sun to shine in the daytime and the moon to shine at nighttime. Let's make pictures of the sun and pictures of the moon.

☼ Joshua, what bright light shines in the day-time sky? God made the sun to keep us warm.

☼ Emily, what light did God put in the nighttime sky? I'm glad God made lights for the day and the night. Kimmie, what is something you would like to thank God for making?

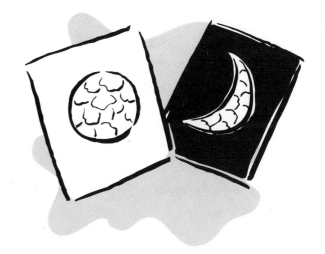

God Made the World

Genesis 1:1-19

In the beginning, there were no tall trees. No flowers. No warm sunshine. There were no animals and no people! Everything was dark.

But God was here. And this is what God did.

First, God said, "Let there be light." And just like that—there was light! God called the light daytime. God made the daytime for working and playing.

God made our world dark part of the time. God called the quiet dark nighttime. God made nighttime for sleeping.

Next, God made the sky. He put this beautiful sky up, up, up high, bright and blue. God made lots of fluffy, puffy white clouds to float in the beautiful blue sky.

Next, God took all the water and put some here and some there until the world had oceans, lakes and rivers full of water.

And between the water was the dry land. God made tall, tall mountains, little round hills and low flat places.

God said, "Let grass and trees and flowers grow." And they did! Soft green grass, tall leafy trees, tiny plants, fruit trees, berry bushes, vegetables and flowers all began to grow. But that's not all God made!

God made special lights—the bright warm sun to shine in the daytime and the moon and the stars to shine at night.

God made everything in our wonderful world. God is SO great!

Shiny Fish

Collect

Bible, large sheet of butcher paper, markers or crayons, foil or metallic wrapping paper, scissors, glue sticks; optional—construction paper.

Prepare

On large sheet of paper, draw a simple underwater scene (sand, seaweed, shells, one or more large fish, etc.). Cut foil or metallic wrapping paper into small squares.

Do

Children glue small squares to fish shape(s) and color underwater scene with crayons or markers. (Optional: Children make individual scenes on separate sheets of construction paper.)

Enrichment Ideas

1. Provide glitter crayons and other shiny materials (large sequins, glitter glue, plastic jewels, etc.) for children to use in creating a glittery underwater scene.

2. Provide watercolors for children to paint their underwater scene.

3. Twist lengths of green crepe paper and glue ends to butcher paper for seaweed.

God Made Animals

Genesis 1:20-25

I can thank God for all the good things He has made.

Talk About

☼ In our Bible story today, God made fish, birds and other animals. Everything God made was just right! Let's make some shiny fish. You can decorate the fish any way you want to.

☼ What colors of fish have you seen? What colors of birds have you seen? God made many different colors of birds and fish.

☼ I'm glad God made fish. Luis, what's one animal you are glad God made? Let's thank God for all the good things He made. Lead children in a brief prayer.

God Made Animals

Genesis 1:20-25

God made our beautiful world! After God made daytime and night-time, He filled the world with oceans and rivers and lakes. He made beautiful plants everywhere. Then God made the sun. He made the moon and stars. God's world was good!

But God's world was VERY quiet. The splashing lakes, rivers and oceans were empty! So God said, "Let the water be full of fish and all sorts of living creatures!" And there were FISH! Big fish and whales and dolphins jumped and swam in the oceans. Bright fish swam near the rocks. In the deepest ocean, fishes that had little lights swam! There were crabs and starfish and sea horses. There were clams that dug themselves into the sand.

Then God looked at the beautiful blue sky. Nothing was there but clouds. So God said, "Let birds fly in the sky." Soon, blue birds and yellow birds, big birds and little birds flew in the sky. They made nests in the trees. Eagles flew high and chickens scratched the ground.

The dry land was full of grass and flowers and trees. But nothing moved there. So God said, "Let there be all kinds of animals." And just as God said, there were animals everywhere! Horses and zebras ran and kicked. Monkeys swung in the trees. Cows, goats and sheep ate the grass. Big gray elephants stomped. Tiny gray mice hid. Big lions roared and tall kangaroos hopped. Dogs and cats ran and played and then slept in the sunshine.

God looked at all the fish and birds and animals He had made. God said, "It is good." God made everything in our world! And He made it just right!

Open the Door

Collect

Bible, construction paper, markers, white paper, scissors, glue.

Prepare

For each child, fold a sheet of construction paper in half widthwise. Draw a doorknob on the outside (see sketch a). Fold white paper and cut out paper dolls (see sketch b), preparing approximately four dolls for each child.

Do

Ask each child to name the people who live with him or her. Give child the appropriate number of paper dolls, cutting additional paper dolls if needed. Children color dolls to represent themselves and the people with whom they live and then glue dolls inside one of the construction-paper sheets you prepared.

Enrichment Ideas

1. Children draw and cut out clothing from colored paper or fabric scraps and glue clothing to their paper dolls.

2. Children glue yarn for hair and wiggle eyes on their paper dolls.

3. Before gluing dolls, older children use paper dolls to act out family situations.

God Made People

Genesis 1:26-31; 2:7-23; 3:20

I can thank God for making me and my family.

Talk About

☀ In our Bible story today, we'll hear about the people in the first family God made. Their names were Adam and Eve. You can each make a picture of the people who are in your family.

☀ Annie, our Bible says that God made you and your family. I'm glad for the people in my family. What are some things you like to do with your family?

☀ Corinne, who are some of the people in your family? Let's thank God for making you and your family.

a.   b.

God Made People

Genesis 1:26-31; 2:7-23; 3:20

God made our wonderful world. God made beautiful birds to fly in the sky. God made fish to swim in the water. God made all kinds of animals on the dry land. God made beautiful flowers and trees to grow everywhere. God put the sun in the daytime sky. He put the moon and stars in the nighttime sky.

But there was no one in the world for God to talk with. And there was no one in the world to take care of what God had made.

Then God made someone to talk to. He made a person. This person was a man. God named the man Adam.

God told Adam to give names to all the living things. So Adam gave just the right name to each one.

Adam was happy with the animals and the trees and the flowers. But there was no other person to talk to Adam. God knew that Adam needed someone to love. Adam also needed help to take care of the beautiful world God had made.

So God made a woman. Adam called her Eve. God said to Adam and Eve, "Take care of the animals and birds and fish that I made. Use the plants for your food."

Adam and Eve must have been glad and thankful for all the good things God had given them. They ate the tasty fruit that grew on the trees. Sometimes in the evening, God came to the garden and talked with Adam and Eve. God loved them very much. And Adam and Eve loved God.

Garden Shapes

God Loves Adam and Eve

Genesis 2:16-17; 3

I can thank God for showing His love by sending Jesus.

Collect

Bible, a variety of pasta shapes (macaroni, penne, etc.), bowls, play dough, plastic knives, toothpicks.

Prepare

Put pasta in shallow bowls.

Do

Children make items found in a garden (flowers, trees, etc.) from play dough, adding details with pasta shapes. Children use plastic knives or toothpicks to add details to play-dough items.

Talk About

☼ In today's Bible story God loved Adam and Eve. He gave them a beautiful garden to live in. God gave Adam and Eve one rule to obey. But they disobeyed God's rule. God still loved them and promised to show His love by sending Jesus. Let's make flowers and trees that we might see in a garden.

☼ Ella, are you making a flower or a tree? What pasta shape can you put on your tree to show branches?

☼ We can thank God for loving us and sending Jesus. Dwight, what else can we thank God for?

Enrichment Ideas

1. Fold several index cards in half to make stand-up cards. On each card draw a simple stick figure. Children use stand-up cards in their play.

2. Children use flower- and fruit-shaped cookie cutters to cut shapes from play dough.

God Loves Adam and Eve

Genesis 2:16-17; 3

God made Adam and Eve a beautiful home in a special garden. The garden was full of fish, birds, animals, flowers and trees. The trees grew delicious food, so Adam and Eve had plenty to eat. There was only one thing they could not do. God told Adam and Eve, "You may eat fruit from all the other trees in the garden, but DO NOT eat from this special tree."

One day, Eve saw beautiful fruit on God's special tree. Eve wanted to eat some of the fruit. She had a choice to make. Eve could choose to obey God, or she could choose to disobey. She reached up into that tree. Eve picked the fruit. Then she ate it. And then Eve gave some to Adam. He ate it, too!

As soon as Adam and Eve had eaten the fruit, they knew they had disobeyed God. They decided to hide.

God called, "Adam, where are you?"

Adam said, "I am hiding because I am afraid." Adam was afraid because he and Eve had eaten from the special tree. They had disobeyed God. God was very sad that Adam and Eve had disobeyed.

God told them they must leave their garden. He told them that many bad things would happen because they had disobeyed. But God never stopped loving Adam and Eve. God gave them a happy promise. Many years later, God kept that promise. God sent His Son, Jesus, to forgive us for the wrong things we do when we don't obey God's rules. God sent Jesus to be our Savior and friend.

Ark Art

Collect

Bible, brown butcher paper, markers, scissors, newspaper, stapler; optional—brown paper bags.

Prepare

On brown butcher paper, draw a large ark (see sketch) that is approximately 2 feet (.6 m) long. Cut two layers of paper to make two ark papers that are the same shape. Make one set of ark papers for each group of four or five children. (Optional: Cut ark shapes from paper bags.)

Do

1. Give two ark papers to each group of four or five children. Children decorate ark papers with markers.

2. When children finish decorating paper arks, staple edges together, leaving one edge open. Children tear and crumple newspaper and use it to stuff paper arks. Staple open side closed.

Enrichment Ideas

1. On one or more classroom walls, attach a long length of white butcher paper. Use masking-tape loops to tape stuffed paper arks to butcher paper. Children decorate butcher paper to make water and draw fish, plants and other things that live in the water.

2. Before class, cut large ark shape from white butcher paper and cut brown construction paper into strips. Children glue strips of paper to ark.

Building the Big Boat

Genesis 6:5-22

God helps me do good things and obey Him.

Talk About

☼ In today's Bible story, Noah obeyed God. Noah built a big wooden ark. An ark is a boat or ship. Let's make some paper arks.

☼ Manny, I can see Rachel needs a new marker. What good thing can you do to help Rachel?

☼ What are some good things we can ask God to help us do? Pray briefly, incorporating the children's answers.

Building the Big Boat

Genesis 6:5-22

After God made the world, more and more people were born. After a long time, there were more people than you could count! But these people did not obey God. They did unkind things to each other, spoiling the beautiful world God had made. This made God sad.

But one man named Noah was different. Noah loved and obeyed God.

God told Noah, "I'm going to cover the world with water to stop all the bad things people are doing."

Then God told Noah, "Build a big boat. I will tell you how to build it." God told Noah which wood to use to build the big boat. God told Noah how tall to build the boat. God told Noah how long to build the boat. God even told Noah where to put the door and window.

God told Noah, "When the water comes, you and your family will be safe in the big boat."

Noah obeyed God. He started building the big boat.

Noah and his family began to cut down trees. Chop! Chop! Chop!

They sawed the wood into boards. ZZZ-zzz-zzz.

They hammered the boards together. Bang! Bang! Bang!

Finally the big boat was finished. It was tall and long.

Noah and his family were glad God helped them know how to build the boat and obey Him. They knew God was taking care of them.

Animal Faces

Collect

Bible, construction paper in a variety of colors, scissors, yarn, paper plates, glue sticks, markers or crayons.

Prepare

Cut geometric shapes (circles, triangles, ovals and rectangles) from construction paper. Cut short lengths of yarn.

Do

Children glue construction-paper shapes and lengths of yarn to paper plates to make animal faces with ears and whiskers. Children may also draw additional facial features.

Enrichment Ideas

1. Children use collage materials, buttons, colored glue and glitter to create animal faces.

2. Cut eye holes in paper plate and staple a tongue depressor to the back of each animal face to create a hand-held mask.

Loading the Big Boat

Genesis 7:1-16

God helps me do good things, even when it's hard.

Talk About

☺ In our Bible story today, God helped Noah load lots and lots of animals into a big boat called an ark. Loading the ark was hard work! Let's make some animals like the ones Noah had on his ark.

☺ We are making some animal faces. Tasha, what animal are you going to make? There were lions in Noah's ark. Tell me some other animals that went in the ark.

☺ What good things can we do while we are making our animals? God helps us do good things. We can thank Him for His help.

Loading the Big Boat

Genesis 7:1-16

Noah and his family built a great big boat, just as God had said to do. But why such a BIG boat? There were only eight people in Noah's family. Here's why the boat had to be so big: God told Noah, "I will bring every kind of animal into the ark to keep them safe."

God also told Noah, "Put food in the boat—lots and lots of food. Food for you and for your family and food for all the animals that will be in the big boat with you." Noah and his family and the animals were going to be in the boat for a long, long time. They would need lots of food. What a big job!

Noah and his family did just what God said to do. They helped each other pack all kinds of food. Then they helped each other put the food into the boat—seed for the birds, and hay and grain for the elephants and mice and cows and horses. What a busy time!

"Now it's time to bring the animals into the boat," Noah told his family. "God wants us to take care of them while we live in the boat."

Hippity-hop, hippity-hop came the two rabbits.

Thump, thump, thump came the two big gray elephants.

Trot, trot, trot came the two horses.

Whoosh flew in many kinds of birds.

Finally, Noah, his family and all the animals and birds were inside the boat. Noah must have been glad God helped him do so many good things!

Rainstorm Pictures

Collect

Bible, several shallow plastic bowls, water, cotton balls, glue, dark-blue construction paper, white chalk.

Prepare

Pour a small amount of water into each bowl.

Do

Children glue cotton balls to papers to make clouds. Children then dip chalk into water and make short chalk marks on papers to depict raindrops.

Safe in the Boat

Genesis 7:17—8:14

I do my best to help others to show I love God.

☼ In our Bible story today, God sent a BIG rainstorm. Noah and his family and many animals were safe in a big boat called an ark. Let's make rainstorm pictures!

☼ Jade, Miguel wants to use the chalk. What can you do to help him? You helped Miguel by handing him the chalk. You really know how to help others.

☼ While it was raining, Noah and his family did good things in the ark. They took care of the animals in the ark. What jobs do you think they did? They must have worked hard!

Enrichment Ideas

1. Children use spray bottles to spray a light mist on their papers and then draw with dry chalk.

2. Children cut tinsel into short lengths for raindrops and glue on papers.

Safe in the Boat

Genesis 7:17—8:14

God brought all the animals and birds into the big boat. Then Noah and his family got into the big boat, too. Pretty soon they began to hear something.

Pitter-pat. Pitter-pat. Soft, gentle rain! God made the rain to come.

Soon it rained harder and harder. The water splashed against the sides of the big boat. But Noah and his family were warm and dry inside the big boat. God was taking care of them. Rain came down for many, many days.

Noah and his family had work to do. They helped each other give hay to the horses and elephants. They scattered grain and seed for the birds to eat. They gave all the animals and birds cool water to drink.

And every morning, Noah and his family helped each other milk the cows and goats. They gathered the eggs the chickens had laid. And all the time, it rained.

Finally the rain stopped! But water covered all the land and bushes and trees. It took days and days and days for the earth to dry. One day Noah sent a bird out through the window of the boat. The bird came back to the boat because it could not find a dry place to land.

A few days later, Noah sent this bird out again. This time the bird came back with a brand-new leaf in its beak. That meant the bird had found a tree. The water was almost all gone.

Noah sent the bird out again. This time the bird did not come back. It had found a dry place to live. That meant the water was gone. God had taken care of Noah and his family and all the animals.

Rainbow Streamers

Collect

Bible, large white paper plates, scissors, crepe-paper streamers in several rainbow colors, measuring stick, stapler, markers.

Prepare

Cut each paper plate in half and then cut off rim. Make one plate for each child. Cut streamers into 18-inch (45.5-cm) lengths.

Do

Help children staple several streamers to one end of plate. Children decorate plates with markers and wave completed rainbow streamers in the air.

God Sends a Rainbow

Genesis 8:15-22; 9:8-17

God helps me do good things, and I can thank Him for His help.

Enrichment Ideas

1. Help children arrange streamers in rainbow order (red, orange, yellow, green, blue, purple).

2. Children use glitter and puff paints to decorate their plates.

3. Play a cassette or CD of children's music. Children wave streamers in the air while music plays.

Talk About

☼ In our Bible story today, Noah, his family and all the animals left the ark to live on dry land. Noah thanked God for keeping them safe during the flood. God put a rainbow in the sky as a reminder of His love. Let's make some rainbow streamers.

☼ Annie, I see you shared the red marker with your sister Corinne. Thank you for doing a good thing. What other good things can you do to help your sister?

☼ I'm thankful God helps me do good things. Ruben, what good thing does God help you to do? Let's thank Him for helping us do good things.

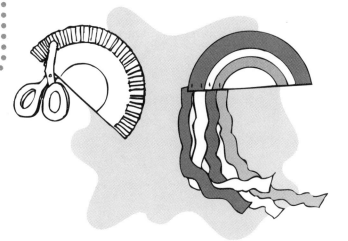

God Sends a Rainbow

Genesis 8:15-22; 9:8-17

Noah and his family and all the animals had been living in the big boat for many days! It had rained and rained and rained! But now the rain had stopped. The water had dried up. It was time to leave the boat.

Noah opened the big door in the side of the boat. Then Noah brought the animals off the boat. Thump-thump-thump-thump. Out came the elephants waving their trunks. Hippity-hop, hippity-hop, hippity-hop came the floppy-eared rabbits. The woolly lambs said "Baa-baa" as they skipped out the door.

Trot, trot, trot came the horses. And the birds flew high, high up in the sky.

Noah and his family walked out of the boat. They stretched and breathed the clean fresh air.

Noah said, "God was good to care for us. We will give God thanks." Together, Noah and his family prayed, "Thank You, God, for caring for us in the big boat."

Then God made a very special promise. God said, "I will NEVER again cover the whole earth with water. I will put a rainbow in the sky to remind everyone of My promise." And God did just that—He put a brightly colored rainbow up in the sky. Noah, his family and all the animals could see it!

Noah and his family remembered God's promise every time they saw a rainbow! Today when we see a rainbow, we can remember God's promise, too. We can remember God's love and help.

Puppet Faces

Collect

Bible, yarn in various hair colors, ruler, scissors, lunch-sized paper bags, markers, glue; optional—wiggle eyes.

Prepare

Cut yarn into 4- to 8-inch (10- to 20.5-cm) lengths. Make a sample puppet.

Do

Children draw their faces and clothing on paper bags. Children glue yarn lengths onto bags for hair. (Optional: Children glue wiggle eyes to faces.) Children use completed puppets to say, "I can obey God."

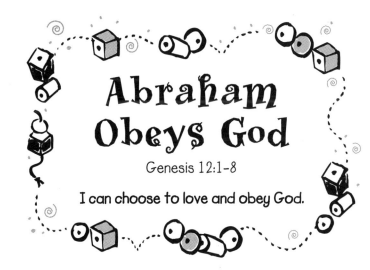

Abraham Obeys God

Genesis 12:1-8

I can choose to love and obey God.

Enrichment Ideas

1. Ask children to identify and choose the color of yarn that matches their hair color.

2. Provide a variety of small fabric squares. Children glue fabric squares onto puppets for clothing.

3. Older children may use puppets to tell ways of obeying God (helping, telling the truth, saying kind words, etc.).

Talk About

☺ In today's Bible story, God told Abraham to move to a new home. Abraham obeyed God. Let's make some puppets of ourselves. You can use your puppet to say, "I can obey God."

☺ Bryan, thank you for helping Ashton glue on his yarn. Helping is a way to obey God. What are some other ways you can help others?

☺ Mona, I see you are being kind by picking up the yarn from the floor. Thank you for choosing to love and obey God. What are some other ways we can be kind in our classroom?

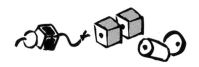

Abraham Obeys God

Genesis 12:1-8

God had a special plan for a man named Abraham. One day God said to Abraham, "Abraham, I want you to move to a new land. I will show you how to get there."

Abraham told his wife, Sarah, and his nephew Lot, "We are going to walk to a new land. God will show us how to get there."

What a busy time! Abraham and Lot had many sheep, goats, cows, camels and donkeys. And they had many helpers to take care of all those animals.

The helpers filled water bags with water for the animals and people to drink along the way.

Sarah and her helpers packed food for the long trip. Everyone helped roll the tents into big bundles.

And then, Abraham, Sarah, Lot and all their helpers and all their animals started out on their long trip to a new land. Step-step-step. Day after day they walked.

Each night they had to carefully unroll their tents and set them up. Then every morning they took down the tents and rolled them up again. It was a big job! But they knew God was taking care of them.

Finally, after many days of walking, God told Abraham, "This place will be your new home."

Abraham and his helpers put up the tents. They found places for all the animals. Then Abraham thanked God for bringing him and all the people with him safely to the new land. God was glad that Abraham obeyed Him.

U-Shaped Sheep

Collect

Bible, white and black construction paper, scissors, markers, glue, cotton balls.

Prepare

For each child, fold white paper in half widthwise. On the fold, round the corners; opposite the fold, cut out an upside down U to make sheep body and legs (see sketch). Save cutout paper for the sheep's head. From the black paper, cut out two ear shapes for each child.

Do

To make sheep, children draw eyes and nose on the head, glue ears to head, glue head to body and then glue cotton balls to the body.

Enrichment Ideas

1. Children curl white strips of paper around pencils to make paper curls. Children glue curls to sheep.

2. Before class, mix the glue and water together in paper bowls (two parts water to one part glue). In class, children roll cotton balls in glue and water mixture and stick on sheep. Children sprinkle glitter over cotton balls to create sparkly sheep.

3. Help children use paper fasteners to fasten sheep's head to body and then make the head move up and down.

Lot Chooses First

Genesis 13

I can choose to be kind to others.

Talk About

☼ In our Bible story, Abraham and Lot had many, many sheep. It was so crowded that their helpers argued about whose grass was whose! They decided to move away from each other. Abraham let Lot choose the land he wanted. Abraham was kind by giving Lot first choice. Today we are going to make some sheep.

☼ Jessica, I see Timothy being kind to you by waiting his turn to use the glue. How can you be kind to Timothy?

☼ Thank you, Aishia, for sharing some cotton balls with David. Choosing to obey is a way to show love. What are some other things you and David can share?

Lot Chooses First

Genesis 13

Abraham and Lot lived with their families in tents. Abraham and Lot had many helpers who lived near them in more tents. And Abraham and Lot had many, many cows and donkeys and sheep and goats and camels. Everywhere you looked there were people and animals.

Every day Abraham's helpers and Lot's helpers took the animals to eat green grass and to drink cool water.

Then one day there was not enough grass to eat or enough water to drink for all their animals. The helpers began to argue.

"We must stop this arguing. We need to move away from each other to find enough grass and water for all our animals," Abraham said. So Lot and Abraham climbed to the top of a hill. They could see far, far away.

Abraham said, "You may choose first, Lot. You may choose the land you want."

Lot pointed to good land, where there was plenty of water and grass. "I'll move to that land," Lot said.

Lot took his family and his helpers and his animals to live in the good land.

Abraham took his family and his helpers and his animals and walked to another place to live. His animals would have enough water and grass, too. God knew that Abraham was kind to Lot. God promised to take care of Abraham. Abraham was glad he had been kind.

Paper Tents

Collect

Bible, white paper, markers, ruler; optional—toy people.

Prepare

For each child, fold a sheet of paper to make a tent (see sketch).

Do

Children unfold and color their tents. (Optional: Older children draw stripes on tents.) Help children refold tents. Children place their tents together to form a community of tents. (Optional: Children use toy people to play with tents.)

Enrichment Ideas

1. Provide toy animals for children to use in their play.

2. Provide additional materials for children to use in decorating tents (stickers, rubber stamps and stamp pad, etc.).

Isaac Is Born

Genesis 17:15-19; 18:1-15; 21:1-8

I can believe God keeps His promises.

Talk About

☼ Today's Bible story tells about Abraham and Sarah. God kept His promise and gave Abraham and Sarah a baby boy named Isaac. Abraham, Sarah and Isaac lived in a tent. Let's make some tents!

☼ Nathaniel, what is a promise? A promise is something you say you will do and then you do it! God always keeps His promises.

☼ Abraham and Sarah were glad when their baby was born. They were glad God kept His promise. God promises to love us. Gabriel, what has God given to you to show He loves you?

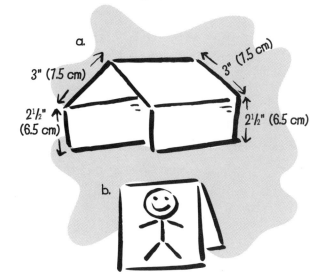

a.

3" (7.5 cm)   3" (7.5 cm)

2¹/₂" (6.5 cm)   2¹/₂" (6.5 cm)

b.

Isaac Is Born

Genesis 17:15-19; 18:1-15; 21:1-8

Abraham was a very old man. His wife, Sarah, was very old, too. They had no children. One day Abraham heard God's voice speaking to him. He was surprised! "Abraham," God said, "I am going to send a baby boy to you and Sarah." Abraham laughed to himself. *A baby boy?* he thought. God said. "Yes! You and Sarah will have a son. You will name your baby Isaac."

One day Abraham saw one, two, three men coming to his tent. These visitors looked like men, but one was really God! The other two were angels. Abraham hurried to invite them in. "Please stay awhile," Abraham said. "Come and rest in the shade! I'll bring water and food."

Abraham said to Sarah, "Please make some bread—quickly!" Sarah baked loaves of bread. Abraham got meat and a helper cooked it. Abraham served the food to his visitors in the shade of his trees.

The visitors ate. Then God said to Abraham, "Next year, your wife, Sarah, will have a baby boy." Sarah was behind the tent door. She was listening. *A baby?* she thought. *How can two old people have a baby?* She laughed!

God heard Sarah laugh. "Abraham," He asked, "why did Sarah laugh? Doesn't she know? I can do anything! Nothing in the whole world is too hard for Me to do. You and Sarah will have a son!"

Abraham and Sarah did have their own baby boy—just as God promised! Abraham and Sarah were very happy. They named their baby Isaac. Abraham and Sarah had a big party to celebrate Isaac's birth. Many, many times Abraham and Sarah must have thanked God for Isaac. God had done just what He promised!

Geometric Camels

Eliezer Prays
Genesis 24

I can pray to God everywhere I go.

Collect

Bible, construction paper in a variety of colors, scissors, clothespins or craft sticks, glue; optional—craft foam.

Prepare

Cut some of the construction paper into at least one large rectangle, one small rectangle and two triangles for each child. (Optional: Instead of construction paper, cut shapes from craft foam.)

Do

Children glue shapes onto papers to make camel pictures, adding clothespins or craft sticks for legs.

Enrichment Ideas

1. Children add yarn or fake fur to camel pictures for texture.

2. Give children additional paper and shapes and invite them to create different animals.

Talk About

☼ In our Bible story today, Eliezer went on a long, long trip. He did not have a car. He rode a camel, and he took nine more camels to carry all the things for his trip. Let's make camel pictures to remind us of his trip.

☼ When Eliezer was on his trip, he prayed to God. He asked God to help him. Where do you like to go? You can pray to God at the park. I'm glad we can pray to God everywhere we go.

☼ Kevin, when you went on a trip, how did you travel? God hears you when you pray in an airplane.

Eliezer Prays

Genesis 24

Abraham was very old. His son Isaac wasn't a baby anymore. Isaac was now a grown man!

It was time for Isaac to be married. Abraham told his helper, Eliezer (ehl-ee-EE-zuhr), "Go to the land where my family lives. Find a good wife for Isaac."

Eliezer was glad to help Abraham and Isaac. He traveled a long, long way. He and his camels were tired and thirsty. So Eliezer stopped his camels by a well of water.

Eliezer climbed down from his camel and prayed, "Dear God, please help me find a kind wife for Isaac."

Just then a young woman named Rebekah came to the well. She was carrying a water jar. "May I have a drink of your water?" Eliezer asked her.

"Yes," said Rebekah. She lowered her jar down, down into the well.

She gave Eliezer a drink. While he was drinking, Rebekah said, "I will also give water to your camels."

What a kind woman Rebekah was! Eliezer thanked her for the water. Then he went to meet her family. He gave them many gifts from Abraham and Isaac and asked if Rebekah would go with him to marry Isaac. Rebekah said, "Yes."

Eliezer prayed and thanked God for helping him find a kind woman to be Isaac's wife. The next day, Eliezer and Rebekah started on the long trip back to Isaac's home.

Two Faces

Collect

Bible, glue, a variety of collage items (yarn, Styrofoam peanuts, beans, macaroni, etc.), small paper plates.

Do

Each child glues collage items to two paper plates to make faces representing Jacob and Esau. Encourage children to make the faces look different from each other.

Jacob and Esau

Genesis 25:19-28

God made the people in my family and He wants us to love each other.

Talk About

☼ Today in our Bible story, we'll hear about two boys, Jacob and Esau. When the boys were born, their parents were glad! Jacob and Esau were twins, but they were very different from each other. You can make your paper-plate faces look different from each other.

☼ Jacob and Esau were brothers. Katy, do you have a brother or sister? God made you and your sister. God wants you and your sister to love each other.

☼ Keisha, I see you are gluing beans on the face to make eyes. What color eyes do you have? What color eyes does your mom have? God made the people in our families. He wants the people in our families to love each other.

Enrichment Ideas

1. Children cut pieces of paper for facial features and hair. Children glue facial features to paper plates.

2. Children glue yarn on plates for hair, eyebrows and beards.

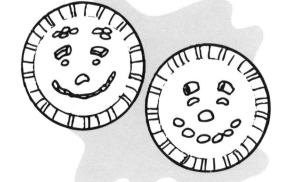

Jacob and Esau

Genesis 25:19-28

Isaac was a man who loved God. Isaac married a lady named Rebekah. For a long time, they had no children. Isaac prayed to God. He asked God to give him children.

God answered Isaac's prayer. God told Rebekah she was soon going to have twin babies. Isaac and Rebekah were going to have TWO babies!

Finally it was time for the babies to be born. The twins were both boys, but they were very different from each other. The older baby was very red. He had lots of hair. His name was Esau.

The other baby was named Jacob. He had smooth skin. He didn't have a lot of hair. These boys were VERY different from each other.

As Esau and Jacob grew up, they still were very different from each other. They looked different from each other. They acted differently from each other.

Esau became a good hunter. He used a bow and arrow to find food for his family to eat. Esau liked to be outdoors. Isaac was very proud of his big, strong son, Esau.

Jacob liked to stay home in the tents where his family lived. He liked to cook good food for his family. His mother, Rebekah, was very proud of her quiet, helpful son, Jacob.

Isaac and Rebekah were very happy that God gave them two sons to love.

Soup Collages

Collect

Bible, construction paper, marker, a variety of dried beans and lentils, small plastic bowls, glue.

Prepare

For each child, draw a large bowl on a sheet of construction paper. Place dried beans and lentils in separate bowls.

Do

Children glue beans and lentils to inside of drawn bowls to make soup collages.

An Unfair Trade

Genesis 25:27-34

I can show love to my family by being kind.

Talk About

☺ Today in our Bible story, we'll hear about two brothers named Jacob and Esau. One day when Esau was VERY hungry, Jacob was not kind to Esau. Jacob did not want to give Esau any of his good-tasting stew. Jacob's stew was a soup made from beans. We are making bean soup pictures.

☺ Sandy, I see you have a lot of beans. Thank you for sharing with your friend Misty. Sharing is a way to be kind. What other things can you share in our class? At home?

☺ Jason, Mandy can't reach the glue. What can you do to be kind to her? Thank you for giving the glue to Mandy. Thank you for being kind. Who in your family shows love to you by being kind?

Enrichment Ideas

1. Instead of beans, children glue different kinds of dry cereal to soup bowls.

2. Provide small paper bowls and invite children to glue beans and lentils to the inside of their bowls.

An Unfair Trade

Genesis 25:27-34

Isaac and Rebekah had two sons, Jacob and Esau. The brothers liked to do very different things. Esau liked to be outdoors. He liked to hunt with a bow and arrow to find food. Jacob did not like hunting. He stayed home and helped his mother, Rebekah.

Esau had been born before Jacob. That meant that one day Esau would be the family's leader. He would also be given most of the things his father, Isaac, owned. Jacob would only get half as much as Esau. Jacob must have thought that was not fair.

The boys grew to be men. One day, Esau went hunting and was gone a long time. When he got home, he was tired and very hungry! He could smell good food cooking.

Jacob was stirring a pot of stew. Esau said, "Give me some of that stew!"

Jacob did not want to share his stew. He said to Esau, "I'll give you stew, but first, you have to make me a promise. Promise me that I can be the family's leader."

Esau smelled the stew. He was hungry. All he could think about was getting food to eat. He said, "I'm going to die if I don't get some food. You can be the leader of the family. Now give me some stew!" Now Esau would not be the family leader. He would not get more of his father's gifts than Jacob.

Jacob knew the trade was not fair, but he did not care. Jacob wanted to be the family leader. He wanted to get most of his father's gifts. And Jacob didn't care that he had been unkind to his own brother. Instead of being unkind like Jacob, God wants us to show love and be kind to the people we live with.

Play-Dough Wells

Collect

Bible, play dough; optional—picture of Bible-times well.

Do

Give each child a fist-sized amount of play dough. Children break dough into small pieces and roll pieces into balls. Place six to eight balls in a circle and explain, **In Bible times, people got water to drink from deep holes in the ground called wells. Big rocks were put around the top of the well.** (Optional: Show picture of Bible-times well.) Children build wells with the balls.

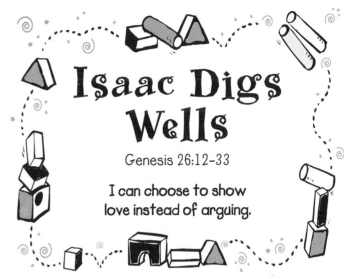

Isaac Digs Wells

Genesis 26:12-33

I can choose to show love instead of arguing.

Talk About

☼ Our Bible story today tells about some wells Isaac's helpers dug. Isaac's neighbors came and said, "These wells are ours." They were unkind to Isaac. But Isaac showed God's love to them. He did not argue. Let's build some wells like Isaac did.

☼ Tyler, thank you for picking up Joe's play dough. You showed God's love. Who are some other people you can show God's love to?

☼ Kirsten, you are helping James build his well. Thank you for working with James. What are some other ways you can show love and help others in our class?

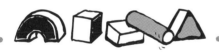

Enrichment Ideas

1. Provide small sandpaper squares, paper and glue. Children glue squares to paper in the shape of a well.

2. Provide small rocks and pebbles. Invite children to press rocks and pebbles into the dough to make stone wells.

3. Use food coloring to make several colors of play dough. Invite children to make colorful wells.

Isaac Digs Wells

Genesis 26:12-33

In Bible times, people did not have sinks and faucets in their homes. People got their water outdoors. They would dip buckets or jars into deep holes in the ground called wells. Isaac needed to dig a well, so his family and his helpers and his animals could have good water to drink. Dig, dig, dig—Isaac's helpers worked hard. The hole got deeper and deeper. Then water began to fill up the hole!

Everyone was happy, EXCEPT Isaac's neighbors. They shouted, "That well is OURS!" They started a big argument. Isaac did not want to argue with his neighbors. So Isaac let them have the well. Isaac moved to another place. He told his helpers to dig another well. Dig, dig, dig—the helpers worked hard. Soon water began to fill up the hole. They had found water again!

But then Isaac's neighbors came again. "That well is OURS!" they shouted. They were very angry. They may have pushed and shoved Isaac's helpers.

Isaac still wanted to be kind to his neighbors. So again Isaac moved to another place. And he told his helpers to dig ANOTHER well. Dig, dig, dig—the helpers worked hard. Soon water began to fill up the hole.

One night soon after, God said to Isaac, "Do not be afraid, Isaac. I will always be with you." Isaac thanked God for being with him.

Isaac's neighbors came again. But this time they did not shout. They said, "We know God is with you. We will not argue with you anymore."

Isaac was very happy! He invited the neighbors to stay for dinner. Isaac was glad God helped him show love.

Family Talk

Jacob's Tricks

Genesis 27:1-45

Telling the truth is a way to show love to my family.

Collect

Bible, index cards, markers, craft sticks, masking tape.

Do

On index cards, children draw the members of their families, one person on each index card. Help children tape cards to craft sticks to make puppets. Using puppets, children act out family situations, showing ways to speak the truth to each other.

Enrichment Ideas

1. Cut index cards into a variety of geometric shapes (squares, circles, triangles, etc.), leaving some cards uncut. Each child chooses two shapes and draws face and hair details on the shapes. Tape a craft stick to the back of each shape.

2. Children glue wiggle eyes onto puppets.

Talk About

☼ In today's Bible story, Jacob did not speak the truth to his father. Jacob's father was sad. Telling the truth helps the people in our families to be happy. Let's make puppets and show ways we can say what is true to the people in our families.

☼ Isabel, who are the people in your family? You can tell the truth to your mom and big brother.

☼ Brad, what could happen if you told your mom you fed the dog when you didn't? Your poor dog would be hungry and sad! It's good to speak the truth to your mom and dad. When are some times you can show love and speak the truth?

Jacob's Tricks

Genesis 27:1-45

One day after Jacob and Esau were all grown up, their father, Isaac, told Esau, "I am getting old. I want to give you my blessing." Isaac wanted to promise Esau that Esau would be the new leader of the family. But first, Isaac asked Esau to go hunting and cook Isaac's favorite food. Esau went out hunting right away!

But Jacob and Esau's mother, Rebekah, wanted Jacob to be the new leader. She told Jacob, "We will get the blessing for YOU while Esau is gone. Do what I say, Jacob."

Isaac was so old that he could not see anything. Rebekah told Jacob to put on Esau's clothes. She put hairy goatskins on Jacob's hands and neck because Esau had a lot of hair. Now that Jacob smelled and felt like Esau, Isaac would think Jacob was Esau! Rebekah made Isaac's favorite meal. She told Jacob to take the food to Isaac.

Jacob took the food to his father. He then said something that was not true. "It's me, Esau," Jacob said. "I've made your food." Isaac asked how he found the food so quickly. "Oh, God helped me!" Jacob lied again!

Isaac said, "It sounds like Jacob's voice, but these hands feel like Esau's hands." Isaac ate, and then he said the words of blessing. Isaac thought he had blessed Esau, but he was really blessing Jacob!

When Esau found out Jacob had not told the truth, he was so angry, he wanted to hurt Jacob! Jacob had to go away and stay with his uncle. He had to stay away for many, many years. Jacob's lies made his family sad and angry. God wants us to show love and tell the truth to our families.

Family Houses

Esau Forgives Jacob

Genesis 32:3-21; 33:1-11

I can show love and forgive the people in my family.

Collect

Bible, 12x18-inch (30.5x45.5-cm) white construction paper, scissors, markers.

Prepare

Fold one paper in half widthwise for each child.

Do

Demonstrate to children how to cut corners off folded paper to form roof (see sketch). Children draw family members inside houses and then draw details on outside of houses (roof, door, windows, etc.).

Talk About

☼ In today's Bible story, Esau was kind to his brother Jacob. Jacob had been unkind to his brother, but Esau loved Jacob and forgave him! Let's make some houses for our families and show the people we can forgive.

☼ Martha, you have many people in your house. How many brothers and sisters do you have? What are their names? What is a way that you can show them love?

☼ We can show love and forgive the people in our families. Ben, what is a way that you can show love to your sister?

Enrichment Ideas

1. Children write house numbers on their houses.

2. Children glue toothpicks on houses to outline walls and roof of houses.

Esau Forgives Jacob

Genesis 32:3-21; 33:1-11

Jacob and Esau were twin brothers, but they were very different from each other. Jacob told lies. He tricked their father, Isaac. He stole important things from Esau. Jacob was afraid Esau would hurt him, so Jacob ran away! He went to live with his uncle for many, many years. He got married and had many children.

But one day, God told Jacob to go back home. Jacob and his family packed their belongings and got ready for the long journey home. Jacob sent some of his helpers to tell Esau that Jacob wanted to come home. The helpers came back and told Jacob, "We went to see Esau. He is coming to meet you. He has 400 men with him!"

Jacob was afraid. Four hundred men sounded like an army! So Jacob prayed. He asked God to keep him and his family safe.

Jacob decided to send Esau some gifts. He sent out a herd of goats. He sent out a flock of sheep and then a herd of camels. He also sent a herd of cattle and a herd of donkeys! Jacob thought if he sent Esau gifts, maybe Esau wouldn't be so angry.

Jacob and his family walked far behind the animals. Finally they could see Esau and his 400 men coming!

Jacob went ahead of his family. As he walked toward Esau, Jacob bowed low, over and over again, to show he was sorry for the wrong things he had done. Esau began to run toward Jacob. *Is Esau going to hurt me?* Jacob must have wondered. Esau came up to Jacob and HUGGED him! Esau had forgiven Jacob!

Colorful Coats

Collect

Bible, brown paper grocery bags, scissors, construction paper in a variety of colors, ruler, tape.

Prepare

Cut grocery bags into shape of Bible-times coats (see sketch). Cut construction paper into 2x5-inch (5x12.5-cm) strips.

Do

Children tape strips of construction paper onto grocery bag coats. Children wear completed coats.

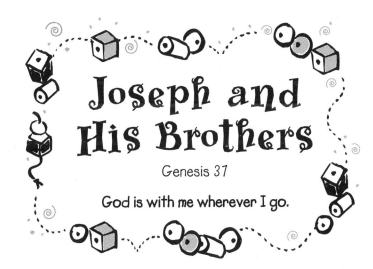

Joseph and His Brothers

Genesis 37

God is with me wherever I go.

Talk About

☼ In our Bible story today, Joseph's father gave Joseph a colorful coat. Joseph's brothers were angry when their father gave Joseph the beautiful coat. They took Joseph's coat and sold him to traders going far away to the country of Egypt. God was with Joseph, even in Egypt. Let's make some colorful coats.

☼ Sean, you have made a beautiful coat. We wear our coats when we go outside. What do you like to do outside? God is with you when you ride your bike outside.

☼ Dana, where do you like to go when you wear your coat? God is with you when you play in the snow.

Enrichment Ideas

1. Children form a repeating color pattern as they attach strips.

2. Children decorate coats by gluing fabric pieces and buttons onto the coats.

Joseph and His Brothers

Genesis 37

Our Bible tells about a boy named Joseph. Joseph had 11 brothers. Joseph and his brothers took care of the family's sheep and watched to make sure no sheep got lost.

Joseph's father was named Jacob. Jacob loved Joseph the best of all his sons. To show that he loved Joseph, Jacob gave him a beautiful coat. But the beautiful coat made his brothers angry!

One day, after caring for the sheep with his brothers, Joseph told his father that his brothers were NOT doing a good job taking care of the sheep. This made Joseph's brothers angrier!

Not long after this, Joseph's brothers took the sheep out to find new grass. They had been gone for a long time. Jacob sent Joseph to find out how they were.

Joseph walked and walked. He looked for his brothers. Joseph's brothers saw him coming a long way off. The brothers remembered how angry they were at Joseph. They made a plan to take Joseph's coat and HURT Joseph!

But the oldest brother said, "Don't hurt him. Just throw him in this deep hole in the ground." And that's just what the brothers did.

Then the brothers noticed some traders coming. (Traders are people who buy and sell things.) One brother said, "Let's SELL Joseph. These traders will take him far, far away." So the brothers sold Joseph to the traders.

Joseph was taken to Egypt, far from his home. He was sold as a slave. (A slave is a person who is owned by someone else.) Joseph must have been very sad. But even though he was far from home, God was with him.

Joseph Puppets

Collect

Bible, paper plates, scissors, pieces of yarn, glue sticks, craft sticks, tape.

Prepare

For every two children, cut a paper plate in half and then cut eye holes in each half.

Do

Children glue yarn to paper-plate halves to make face puppets with hair. Help children tape craft sticks to puppets to make handles. Children hold face puppets so that they can see through the eye holes as you talk about the Bible story.

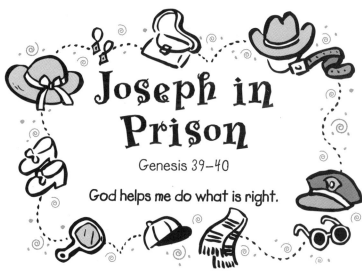

Joseph in Prison

Genesis 39–40

God helps me do what is right.

Enrichment Ideas

1. Children paint hair, eyebrows and nose on paper plates.

2. Provide Bible-times dress-up clothes (robes, fabric strips, sandals, etc.) for children to use with masks while acting out story.

Talk About

☀ In our Bible story today, Joseph worked for a man in Egypt. God helped Joseph do what was right. Later, Joseph was put in jail, even though he had not done anything wrong. Use your face puppet to show me what Joseph's face might have looked like when he was put in jail.

☀ Laura, thank you for picking up the craft sticks. You are doing what is right. What are some other ways to do right?

☀ God was with Joseph and helped him do what was right wherever he was. That must have made Joseph glad! Show me a glad face with your face puppet. What is a right thing that you can do?

Joseph in Prison

Genesis 39—40

Joseph was in Egypt. His brothers had been mean to him and sold him to traders. The traders sold Joseph as a slave. (A slave is a person who is owned by someone else.) Joseph was far away from his family. But God still cared about him.

Joseph was sold to Potiphar (PAHT-ih-fuhr). Joseph worked hard for Potiphar. He did his best work. Soon, Potiphar put Joseph in charge of his house. Joseph was in charge of all Potiphar's helpers and money! But then, Potiphar's wife lied about Joseph. Potiphar put Joseph into JAIL, even though Joseph had not done anything wrong. Joseph decided to keep on doing what was right, even when he was in jail. Joseph knew God loved him.

Joseph worked in the jail. Joseph did a VERY good job. Because Joseph did such good work, the jailer put Joseph in charge of everyone in the jail!

One day Joseph saw a very sad man. The man had been an important helper to the king. He had tasted everything Pharaoh drank to make sure that it was safe. But the king got angry at him and put the man in jail. The man had had a dream that he didn't understand. The man told his dream to Joseph.

"God has helped me know what your dream means," said Joseph. "In three days you will get out of jail. You will work for the king again. When you go back, please ask the king to let me out of here." The man said he would help Joseph.

Three days later the man went back to his old job. But the man forgot all about Joseph! Joseph stayed in jail for a long, long time. But Joseph didn't give up. He knew God was still with him, helping him do what is right.

What's in the Bag?

Collect

Bible, scissors, brown paper grocery bags, precut pictures of foods from magazines or grocery-store advertisements, glue sticks.

Prepare

Make a T-shaped cut in the side of each grocery bag (see sketch a).

Do

Children select pictures of foods and glue them inside grocery bags (see sketch b).

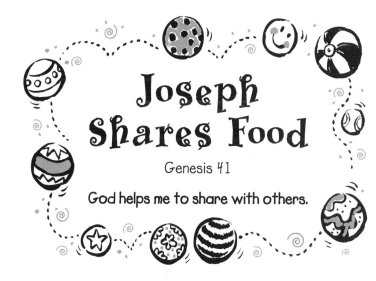

Joseph Shares Food

Genesis 41

God helps me to share with others.

Talk About

☺ In today's Bible story, Joseph helped the people in Egypt. Joseph showed them how to save food so that they could share it with others later, when food was hard to find. Let's make some food bags with pictures of foods that we would like to share with others.

☺ Thomas, you found a picture of an apple. When might you share an apple with someone? What is something else you can share with your brother?

☺ Aurelia, I see you handed Alan some glue. You know how to share! What are some other things you share with your friends?

Enrichment Ideas

1. Older children look through magazines or advertisements to find and cut their own pictures.

2. Children color the outside of their bags and may use inventive spelling to add a name (or logo) of a real or imaginary grocery store.

a.

b.

Joseph Shares Food

Genesis 41

One night, the king of Egypt, called Pharaoh, had a very strange dream. The next morning, Pharaoh told his helpers, "In my dream, seven fat cows came out of the river. And seven skinny cows came out of the river. Then the seven skinny cows ate the fat cows, but they stayed skinny. What could this strange dream mean?"

"Joseph might be able to tell you what your dream means," one of Pharaoh's helpers said. "Bring Joseph to me!" Pharaoh said. When Joseph came, Pharaoh said, "I had a dream, but I don't know what it means. Can you tell me what my dream means?" "No, I can't," Joseph said. "But God will help me know what your dream means." So Pharaoh told Joseph his dream.

Joseph said, "The seven fat cows mean that for seven years we will have more than enough food to eat. The skinny cows mean that after those seven good years, there will be seven hard years with nothing to eat. We need to save our extra food. We can put it in big barns. Then when no food is growing, the people can eat the food we have saved."

Pharaoh told Joseph, "Since God helped you know what my dream meant, I want you to make sure that the extra food is saved."

Joseph told Pharaoh's helpers to build big buildings. For seven years the helpers poured the extra food into sacks. The helpers put the sacks into the big buildings.

After seven years, no food grew at all. "We have no food," the people told Pharaoh. "And we are hungry." Pharaoh told the people to go to Joseph. Then Joseph opened the buildings and sold the food to the people. God helped Joseph make sure all the people had enough food to share.

Heart Windows

Collect

Bible, 12x18-inch (30.5x45.5-cm) red construction paper, scissors, ruler, 5x10-inch (12.5x25.5-cm) white paper, tape, markers.

Prepare

Cut a large heart shape out of red paper and cut 4½x8-inch (11.5x20.5-cm) windows in heart (see sketch). Make one for each child.

Do

Help children tape white paper to back of red hearts. Children open windows and draw pictures of friends or family members on white paper. As children draw, talk about ways to show love to others.

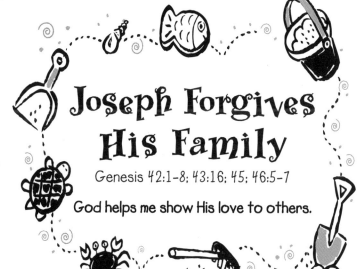

Joseph Forgives His Family

Genesis 42:1-8; 43:16; 45; 46:5-7

God helps me show His love to others.

Talk About

☼ In our Bible story today, Joseph showed God's love to his brothers, even though they had been mean to him. Let's make hearts to remind us to show God's love to others.

☼ Thank you, Todd, for letting Andrea use the tape first. What are some other things you can take turns using in our classroom? Taking turns is a way to show God's love to others.

☼ We show God's love by helping each other. Dina, what are some other ways to help the people in our class?

Enrichment Ideas

1. Children decorate the front of the paper hearts. You may also provide collage materials (lace, wrapping-paper scraps, ribbon, etc.) for children to glue to the front of the hearts.

2. As children tell ways God helps them show His love to others, print their words on the front of their paper hearts.

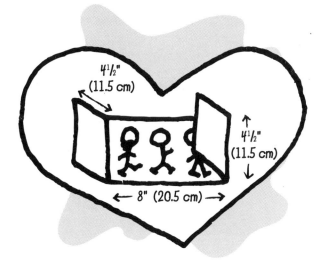

4½" (11.5 cm)

4½" (11.5 cm)

← 8" (20.5 cm) →

Joseph Forgives His Family

Genesis 42:1-8; 43:16; 45; 46:5-7

No food was growing where Jacob and his family lived. They would soon have nothing to eat! Then Jacob heard that he could buy grain in Egypt. Grain was just what Jacob and his family needed to make bread and other good foods.

Jacob said to 10 of his sons, "I want you to go to Egypt and buy some grain for us to eat." Right away the 10 brothers started on their trip to Egypt. When the brothers finally got to Egypt, they went to the leader who was selling grain. They didn't know that this leader was their brother Joseph! The brothers hadn't seen Joseph since he was young. Now he was all grown up. He was dressed like an Egyptian king.

When Joseph looked to see who wanted to buy grain, he was surprised! He knew the men standing in front of him were his very own brothers! "We have come to buy grain," the brothers said to Joseph. Joseph said to his helpers, "Bring these men sacks of grain." The helpers loaded the brothers' donkeys with sacks of grain. The brothers returned home.

But later, Joseph's brothers returned to Egypt because they needed MORE food. This time Joseph told them "I am your brother Joseph." The brothers were very surprised! At first they were afraid. They had been very mean to him. *Will Joseph be mean to us?* they wondered.

But Joseph hugged each of them. "Take plenty of grain home," Joseph said kindly. "Then hurry back here. Bring our father, Jacob. And bring all your families back here to live." Soon Joseph's father and brothers and their families came to live with Joseph. They must have been glad to be together again! Joseph showed God's love to his family.

Basket Weaving

Collect

Bible, 2-foot (.6-m) lengths of yarn, tape, strawberry basket for each child.

Prepare

Wrap one end of each yarn length with tape. Tie the other end of the yarn length to an upper corner of each strawberry basket.

Do

Children make baskets by weaving yarn through sides of strawberry baskets.

Baby in a Basket

Exodus 2:1-10

God shows His care for me by giving me people who love me.

Talk About

☼ In today's Bible story, baby Moses' mother cared for him by making a special basket. Let's make our own special baskets.

☼ I'm glad God gives us people who love us and care for us. Javier, your dad loves and cares for you. What does your dad do to care for you?

☼ Who are some other people who love you? God gives us people who love and care for us. Let's thank God for our families. Pray briefly.

Enrichment Ideas

1. Cut river shapes out of large sheets of blue construction paper. Children glue baskets onto river shapes.

2. Children wrap toy people in pieces of fabric and place them in baskets.

Baby in a Basket

Exodus 2:1-10

Our Bible tells us about a special family. This family had a dad, a mom, a big sister, a big brother and a baby brother. The baby's name was Moses.

Moses' family loved him very much. Moses' family took good care of him. Every day they fed baby Moses. They wrapped baby Moses in soft blankets. Every day they played with baby Moses. God planned for Moses to have a family to care for him.

But there was a mean king who wanted to hurt Moses. Moses' family must have been scared! God helped Moses' mom plan a way to keep her baby safe.

Moses' mom made a special basket. She put soft blankets in the basket. Then she carefully laid Moses in the basket. Moses' mom carried the basket with Moses in it to the river. She placed the basket on top of the water. Moses' big sister stayed with the basket and watched over Moses.

The king's daughter came to the river. The king's daughter wasn't mean. She was kind. She saw the basket. When she opened it, she found Moses crying. "This poor baby," she said. The king's daughter felt sorry for Moses. "This baby needs someone to care for him." Moses' big sister heard this. She went to the king's daughter.

"I will go get someone to care for the baby," Moses' big sister said. Then she ran to get Moses' mom.

Moses' mom took good care of him. The king's daughter made sure the mean king did not hurt the baby. Moses' family was glad God helped them keep Moses safe.

Pack It Up

Collect

Bible, discarded magazines or catalogs, scissors, yarn, ruler, construction paper in a variety of colors, transparent tape, hole punch.

Prepare

From magazines or catalogs, cut out pictures of items to pack in a suitcase, preparing enough pictures so that each child will have several to choose from. Cut two 8-inch (20.5-cm) yarn lengths for each child.

Do

1. Each child tapes together two sheets of construction paper as shown in sketch. In the outside edges of the papers, help children punch two holes. Help children thread a yarn length through each set of holes and tie ends together to form handles.

2. Children select catalog pictures and tape them to the inside of their paper suitcases.

Enrichment Ideas

1. Children decorate the outside of their suitcases with words and pictures cut from a travel brochure, or color suitcases with markers.

2. Instead of making suitcases, children make a collage by taping pictures of things to take on a trip onto a large sheet of butcher paper.

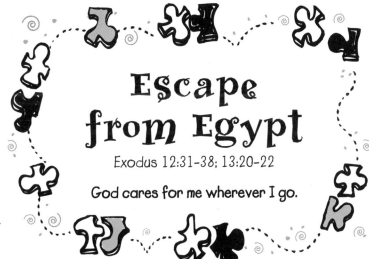

Escape from Egypt

Exodus 12:31-38; 13:20-22

God cares for me wherever I go.

Talk About

☼ In our Bible story today, God's people went on a long trip. Let's pretend we're going on a trip, too. We'll make suitcases to take on our pretend trip.

☼ You have put four things into your suitcase. Where have you gone on a trip? What did you do to get ready for your trip? What did you pack?

☼ Maribel, where do you like to go? I like the park, too. God cares about us when we go to the park. He cares about us wherever we go.

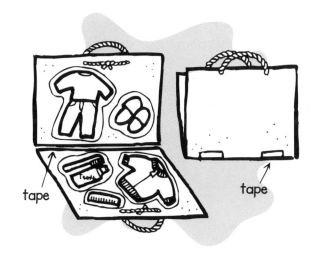

tape

tape

Escape from Egypt

Exodus 12:31-38; 13:20-22

Our Bible tells about a time when God wanted His people to go to a new home far away. God told Moses to be the leader. God said, "I will be with you."

How excited the people were! "We will need food to eat," they said. So moms cooked special food to take on the trip. "And we will need water to drink," they said. So boys and girls filled water bags. "What will we wear and where will we sleep?" they asked. So grandmas tied clothes and blankets into big bundles. "And what about all our animals?" they asked. So dads got the sheep, goats, cows and donkeys ready to go.

Soon it was time to start on the long, long trip. Moses told the people, "God will take care of us. God will lead us and show us the way." And God did that in a very special way. During the day, God put a big white cloud in the sky. The people followed the cloud. During the night, God put fire in the sky. The fire showed the people God was with them.

Step, step, step—moms and dads, aunts and uncles, grandmas and grandpas walked down the road. Step, step, step—boys and girls walked down the road. Clippety-clop, clippety-clop—sheep, goats, cows and donkeys walked down the road. All of the people and animals walked behind God's cloud.

The people were glad they were going to a new home. They were glad God showed them He was with them. The people knew God was taking care of them on their long, long trip.

Shoe-Print Path

Collect

Bible, length of butcher paper, crayons.

Do

1. Help children form pairs and take turns standing on butcher paper as their partner outlines their shoes.

2. Children decorate their shoe prints and then walk on the path, stepping on the shoe prints.

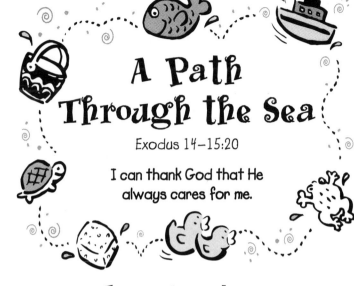

A Path Through the Sea

Exodus 14–15:20

I can thank God that He always cares for me.

Enrichment Ideas

1. Children brush a thin layer of glue inside their footprints and sprinkle sand to create sandy footprints.

2. Paint the bottom of children's feet. Invite them to walk on a length of butcher paper, creating footprints.

Talk About

☼ In today's Bible story, God kept His people safe on a very long trip. He helped them cross a big sea. Let's make shoe prints and pretend we're going on a long trip and crossing a sea.

☼ God cares for us by giving us feet and hands. What can your feet do? What can your hands do? What can other parts of your body do?

☼ We can thank God for caring for us. Lorrie, what do you want to thank God for? That's right! God gives us feet.

A Path Through the Sea

Exodus 14–15:20

God's people were on a long trip. God told Moses where to go and where to stop. Step, step, step–the people walked and walked and walked. Clippety-clop, clippety-clop–the animals also walked and walked and walked. God's people were going to a new home far away.

One day God's people stopped in front of a big sea. They looked around. All they could see was lots and lots of water in front of them. The people felt afraid. They didn't know how to get across the water. There were no boats to ride in. There was no bridge to walk across.

Moses knew the people felt afraid. Moses said, "Don't be afraid. God will help us." Moses held his hand out over the water, just as God told him to do. Then God sent a great big wind to blow the water out of the way. Ooooo! How the wind blew! Ooooo! The wind blew some of the water to one side. Ooooo! The wind blew some of the water to the other side. Right in the middle of the water was a dry path for the people and animals to walk on. They walked all the way to the other side without even getting their feet wet!

Then God told Moses to hold his hand out over the water again. The wind stopped. All the water splashed together again and covered up the dry path. The people were very happy that God had helped them. They sang songs to God. Some women played tambourines. They wanted to show their thanks to God for His care and help.

Pizza Party

Collect

Bible, white paper or poster board, markers (several red and yellow, plus other colors), scissors; optional—yellow and/or white yarn, ruler, glue.

Prepare

Draw a large circle on white paper or poster board and cut out. Make one for each child. (Optional: Cut yellow and/or white yarn into 2- to 3-inch (5- to 7.5-cm) lengths.)

Do

Distribute circles to children. Using markers, children color sauce and toppings (tomatoes, mushrooms, olives, etc.) on their pizza and color the crust. (Optional: Children glue on pieces of yarn for cheese.)

Enrichment Ideas

1. Children cut construction paper into shapes to represent different pizza toppings to be glued on pizzas: black circles for olives, red circles for pepperoni, green strips for peppers, white semicircles for mushrooms, etc.

2. Children glue precut pizza logos onto small boxes and pretend to deliver their pizzas to friends.

A Desert Surprise

Exodus 15:22-25; 16

God shows love to me by giving me food and water.

Talk About

☼ In our Bible story, God gave His people good water and food. God gives us food and water to show His love for us. Let's make pretend pizzas.

☼ Angela, I see that you are drawing tomatoes on your pizza. God loves us and gives us food and water. What else do you like on your pizza?

☼ Pizza is one of my favorite foods. God made tomatoes to grow so that we can have tomato sauce. God makes wheat for flour. Where does cheese come from? I'm glad God made cows and other animals and plants so that we can have good food to eat. What is your favorite food?

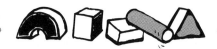

A Desert Surprise

Exodus 15:22-25; 16

God's people were on a long trip. They walked through the desert. The desert is a hot place. There are not many trees for shade. There is not much water to drink, but there is a lot of hot sand. God's people walked across the hot, hot sand. Step-step-step.

For three days, God's people had no water. "We are thirsty!" they all said. Then someone shouted, "Water!" They saw beautiful cool water. The people ran to the water. They took big drinks. Yuk! The water tasted bad! "We can't drink this water," the people said. "Where will we get good water?" they asked Moses.

Moses asked God what to do. God told Moses to throw a special piece of wood into the water. The special piece of wood made the water taste good. Everyone drank the good-tasting water.

God's people had brought food with them from their old home. That food was almost gone. There were no stores to buy more food. "We're hungry," the people said. "What shall we eat?" the people asked Moses. Again Moses talked to God. That night God sent many birds to the people's camp. Now the people had plenty of meat to eat. They were happy.

But God gave them even more. The next morning the ground was covered with little white flakes. "What is it?" the people asked.

"This is the bread God sent," Moses said. The people picked up the bread and tasted it. It was good! The bread was called manna.

God loved and cared for His people. The people thanked God for His gifts of food and water.

Grapevine Art

Collect

Bible, scissors, purple and green construction paper, markers, large sheet of butcher paper, glue.

Prepare

Make grapes by cutting small circle shapes from purple paper. Cut green paper into leaf shapes.

Do

Children draw long curly lines on butcher paper to represent grapevine. Children glue grapes and leaves onto grapevine.

Spies Visit the Promised Land

Numbers 13—14:35

God is with me wherever I go.

Talk About

☺ In our Bible story, we heard about two men named Joshua and Caleb. Joshua and Caleb knew that God would always be with them. When they went to a new land, God gave them lots of good-tasting grapes to eat. Let's make a big grapevine.

☺ Eva, I like the lines you are drawing for our grapevine. Where can you buy grapes? God is with you when you go to the store.

☺ Charlie, where did you go today? I like going out to breakfast, too. We can thank God that He is with us wherever we go.

Enrichment Ideas

1. Instead of drawing a grapevine, children glue brown yarn to paper to make vine.

2. Invite children to cut their own grapes and leaves, or to paint grapes and leaves.

3. Children make individual grapevine pictures.

Spies Visit the Promised Land

Numbers 13–14:35

Moses sent 12 men to explore the land God promised to give the Israelite people. The men secretly looked at the cities and towns. They saw the good food that grew in the land. They saw the people who lived there.

The 12 men came back to Moses. They brought some of the fruit from the Promised Land—a bunch of grapes so big that two men had to carry it! But 10 of the men were scared. They told Moses that the people who lived in the land were too big and strong. They said the cities were too big. They did not think God could help them live in the land.

But two of the men, Joshua and Caleb, knew God would keep His promise to give them the land. "Don't be afraid," they said. "The Lord is with us." But the Israelites didn't believe Joshua and Caleb.

God told Moses that because the people did not trust Him, they would not be able to go to the Promised Land for a long time. The people would have to live in the desert for many more years. But God promised Joshua and Caleb would get to live in the Promised Land because they trusted God. Joshua and Caleb knew that God would be with them wherever they went.

River Pictures

Crossing the Jordan

Joshua 3—4:18

When I am afraid, God helps me.

Collect

Bible, 12x18-inch (30.5x45.5-cm) sheets of white construction paper, markers, blue collage materials (ribbon, yarn, fabric pieces, etc.), glue.

Prepare

For each child, draw a river outline on a sheet of construction paper.

Do

Children glue collage materials to river outline to make river pictures. (Optional: Children draw fish swimming in the river.)

Talk About

☺ In today's Bible story, God's people needed to cross a big river. There was lots of water in the river. The people were afraid to try to cross the river. God helped the people. He stopped the river so that His people could walk across on dry ground. Let's make some river pictures.

☺ Robin, I see that you are letting Kasey use the glue first. Thank you for helping. You are a good friend. God helps us by giving us friends.

☺ God is with us when we are afraid. Rebecca, when is a time it would be good to remember that God helps us?

Enrichment Ideas

1. Thin glue with water and then add blue food coloring. Children use paintbrushes to paint blue glue onto papers before adding collage materials.

2. Give children watercolor paints or food coloring mixed with water to paint a picture of their river.

3. Children cut stones from brown, black or gray paper to glue onto their river pictures.

Crossing the Jordan

Joshua 3—4:18

God's people were glad! They were almost to the new land God was going to give them. They were camped by a river. The new land was on the other side of that river.

Joshua was their leader. He told the people God's instructions. "Get ready. Tomorrow God will do amazing things!"

The people got ready. But then they looked at the river. The water moved fast. It looked scary! No one could swim across that fast river! How would they cross the river and get to the new land?

God had told Joshua just what to do. When it was time to cross the river, Joshua said, "Follow God's leaders!" The leaders, called priests, came to the edge of that rushing river. The priests' feet touched the water. Then something amazing happened! The water stopped rushing by! All the water stopped far away from where the people were standing. The people could see the water. It was standing up in a big wall!

"God did this!" the people shouted. "We can walk across! Thank You, God!"

All of God's people walked across the riverbed. Their feet didn't even get muddy! As they walked across, each family leader picked up a big stone from the riverbed.

The priests stepped out of the riverbed last. And then, WHOOSH! The water came rushing back! God's people stacked up the stones they had taken from the riverbed. Whenever the people saw those stones, they remembered how God had helped them cross the river. They told how God had made the water stand up like a wall. They told about God's power and help!

Blow Your Horn

Collect

Bible, yarn, scissors, measuring stick, 9x12-inch (23x30.5-cm) sheets of construction paper, markers, tape, hole punch.

Prepare

Cut yarn into 24-inch (61-cm) lengths. Cut paper as shown in sketch a.

Do

Give each child a sheet of construction paper. Children color and draw designs on their paper. Roll each paper into a horn shape and tape closed. Cut each horn as shown in sketch b. Punch two holes near top of horn, thread length of yarn through holes and tie so that children can hang horns around their necks.

Enrichment Ideas

1. Cut construction paper into small pieces. Children glue pieces onto their horns.

2. Make horns from black paper. Provide gel pens for children to color their horns.

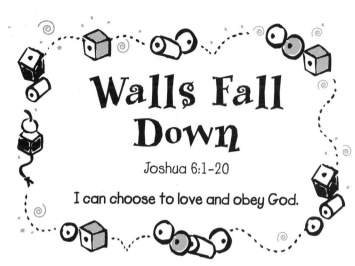

Walls Fall Down

Joshua 6:1-20

I can choose to love and obey God.

Talk About

☼ In our Bible story today, the Israelites obeyed God when He asked them to march around Jericho and blow their horns. Let's make some horns that we can blow.

☼ Pam, thank you for putting away the yarn. You are obeying when you help others. What are some other ways you can help others?

☼ It is good to love and obey God. We can obey by being kind. Let's name some ways we can show our love for God by being kind.

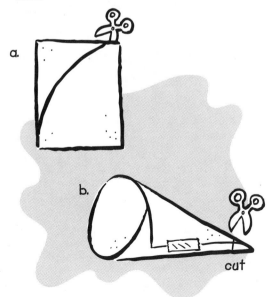

a.

b.

cut

Walls Fall Down

Joshua 6:1-20

Joshua and the Israelites were in the land God had promised them. They were camped outside the city of Jericho. All around the city there was a huge wall made of rocks. The people of Jericho closed the gates to their city. They did not let anyone in or out. They were afraid of the Israelites, but they felt safe behind their city's big wall.

God told Joshua that the Israelites would take over the city of Jericho. God told Joshua what to do. Joshua and the Israelites did just what God said.

All of the Israelite men marched in a long line near the city wall. Some of the priests marched with them. The priests carried the box that held God's laws. Other priests blew on horns as they marched. They marched one time all the way around the city wall. That's all they did for six days!

Then on the seventh day, the Israelites marched around the wall seven times. Then they stopped. The priests blew the longest, loudest blasts they could make on their horns. And Joshua led the people to shout with loud voices!

As the Israelites shouted, CRASH! The wall around the city fell flat to the ground! The Israelites marched straight into the city. God had helped the Israelites take over Jericho, just as God had promised. The Israelites loved God. They were glad they had obeyed Him.

Mud Paintings

Collect

Bible, water, white glue, paper cups, dirt, plastic spoons, newspaper, paintbrushes, white paper or construction paper.

Prepare

Make mud paint. Mix equal parts water and white glue in a cup. Add dirt to water and glue mixture and stir with plastic spoon. Continue adding dirt and stirring until mixture is the consistency of thick paint. Prepare one cup of mud paint for every three children. Cover work area with newspaper.

Do

Children paint with mud paint on paper.

Enrichment Ideas

1. Help older children mix their own mud paint and then paint pictures of things they can share to obey God's Word.

2. Children finger-paint using mud paint.

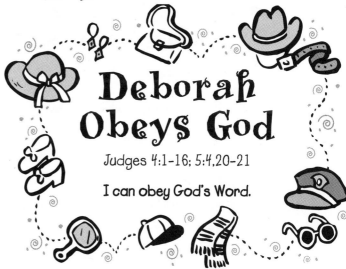

Deborah Obeys God

Judges 4:1-16; 5:4,20-21

I can obey God's Word.

Talk About

☼ In our Bible story, a woman named Deborah listened to God and obeyed Him. God helped Deborah. God sent a huge rainstorm. The rain made lots of mud, and all the chariots got stuck in the mud. The soldiers ran away! Let's paint with mud to help us remember this story.

☼ Kevin, I see you are painting a mountain. I like to go camping in the mountains. What is a way to obey God by helping someone when you are camping?

☼ Thank you for taking turns with the cup of mud paint. Taking turns is a way to obey God by being kind. What is something else you can take turns using?

Deborah Obeys God

Judges 4:1-16; 5:4,20-21

Deborah was a woman who loved God and listened to Him. God told Deborah messages to give to His people. God loved His people, but they were not obeying Him or praying to Him. Because they disobeyed God, the people had big trouble! An army with many soldiers and 900 chariots wanted to fight them! (A chariot is a cart pulled by a horse.) The leader of the army was named Sisera.

Finally, the people of Israel remembered to pray to God. God gave Deborah a message for a man named Barak (BEHR-uhk). Deborah told Barak, "God has an important job for you. God says: 'Take 10,000 men to Mount Tabor. I will bring Sisera with his chariots and army to the river there. I will help you get rid of Sisera.'"

But Barak was afraid! Barak said, "Deborah, if you go with me, I will go. But if you don't go, I won't go." Deborah wanted Barak to trust God and obey. "I will go with you," she said.

Soon 10,000 men went with Barak and Deborah up Mount Tabor. Sisera was getting ready to fight, too. He and his army rode toward Mount Tabor. Sisera was sure he would win. But Sisera didn't know the Israelites had GOD'S help!

Deborah and Barak looked down from the mountain. They could see out across the big flat land. The chariots were coming closer and CLOSER. Soon the whole valley was FULL of chariots!

"Go!" Deborah said to Barak. "God will help you. You will win!"

Barak and his men started down the mountain. Just then, God sent a rainstorm! The chariots must have gotten stuck in the mud! Sisera and his men ran away from their stuck chariots. Barak's army chased them until there was no one left to chase! Deborah and Barak were glad they had obeyed God.

Cereal Pictures

Collect

Bible, dry cereal in a variety of colors and shapes (no flakes), bowls, paper, marker, glue, construction paper.

Prepare

Place cereal in separate bowls. Post a note alerting parents to the use of food in this activity. Also check registration forms for possible food allergies.

Do

Children glue cereal pieces onto construction paper in designs of their own choosing. Children eat leftover cereal.

Ruth Loves Naomi

Ruth 1—2:23

I can show love for others by being kind and patient.

Talk About

☼ In today's Bible story, Ruth gathered grain to make food for herself and Naomi. Grains are little seeds used to make foods like breads and cereal. Let's make pictures with cereal.

☼ Amanda, thank you for sharing the cereal. Sharing is a way to be kind. What are some other things you can share?

☼ Justine, if you want to use the glue, what do you need to do? You can ask Stefan to hand you the glue. Thank you for waiting patiently to use the glue.

Enrichment Ideas

1. Children glue cereal pieces in a repeating pattern. For example, children place one square piece and then two round pieces, repeating the pattern as they make their designs.

2. Before class, draw simple shapes on sheets of construction paper. In class, children choose shapes to outline and/or fill in with cereal.

Ruth Loves Naomi

Ruth 1—2:23

Our Bible tells about two women who loved and obeyed God. Their names were Ruth and Naomi. Ruth and Naomi did not have any money to buy food. They were hungry, so Ruth went to find some food.

Ruth went to a field where workers were cutting grain. The grain was used to make bread. The workers tied the grain into bundles. Some of the grain fell on the ground. The workers left the grain on the ground to be picked up by people who did not have enough food to eat. Ruth asked one of the workers if she could pick up some of the grain from the ground. He said, "Yes." So Ruth picked up the grain and put it into her basket. She worked and worked.

A man named Boaz owned the field. He saw Ruth working hard. Boaz told Ruth, "From now on you may pick up all the leftover grain you can find in my field. And when you are thirsty, you may drink from our water jars." Boaz was kind to Ruth.

Later that day, Boaz brought some food to Ruth. She was hungry, but she didn't eat it all. She saved some food to take home to Naomi. Then Ruth went back to work. She picked up all the grain she could carry in her basket. At night, she went home.

Naomi was surprised that Ruth brought home so much grain. There was enough to make many loaves of bread. Ruth gave Naomi the food she had saved for her. Naomi was glad that Ruth was loving and kind to her. She was glad that Boaz was kind, too.

Coat Collages

Collect

Bible, 9x12-inch (23x30.5-cm) sheet of construction paper for each child, marker, 2-inch (5-cm) construction paper squares, glue; optional—2-inch (5-cm) fabric squares.

Prepare

Draw a coat outline on each child's paper.

Do

Children make collages of Samuel's coat by gluing squares to coat outlines. (Optional: Children glue fabric squares to outlines.)

Enrichment Ideas

1. Provide squares in two or three colors. Children glue squares onto coat in a repeating pattern.

2. Children use wallpaper pieces to decorate coats.

3. Cut a large paper-doll shape for each child. Children glue coats onto Samuel paper dolls.

Hannah's Prayer

1 Samuel 1; 2:18-19

I talk to God to show my love for Him and to ask for His help.

Talk About

☼ The Bible tells about a woman named Hannah. Hannah asked God to send her a baby boy. God did! Hannah named the baby Samuel. Every year Hannah made a coat for Samuel to wear. Today we're going to make coats.

☼ Carole, there are many colors in your coat. What is your favorite color? What are some other colors you like?

☼ Hannah prayed to God because she loved Him. We pray to God to show our love for Him, too. What are some things you ask God to help you do?

Hannah's Prayer

1 Samuel 1; 2:18-19

Hannah and her husband, Elkanah (ehl-KAA-nuh), loved each other and God very much. But Hannah and Elkanah had no children. Hannah felt very sad.

Hannah and Elkanah went to a special place to worship God. The special place was called the Tabernacle. Hannah prayed to God, "Dear God, please give me a baby boy. When he is old enough, I will bring him to the Tabernacle to be Your helper."

Eli lived at the Tabernacle. He prayed to God and taught others about God. "I pray God gives you what you ask," Eli told Hannah. Hannah and Elkanah went home.

After many, many days, a baby boy was born to Hannah. Hannah named the baby Samuel. Every day Samuel grew taller and stronger. Hannah took good care of little Samuel. She cooked good food for him to eat. She made clothes for him to wear. And best of all, Hannah taught little Samuel about God.

Finally, the day came when Samuel was big enough to go to the Tabernacle. Hannah, Elkanah and Samuel went to the Tabernacle. Samuel stayed there with Eli to learn to be God's helper, just as his mother, Hannah, had promised.

Every year Samuel's mother made a special new coat for him. And every year she had to make a bigger and bigger coat! Do you know why? Because Samuel GREW, just like you do. And as he grew a little taller and a little stronger, Samuel also grew to love God! Hannah was glad Samuel was her son. And Hannah was glad she had prayed to God.

Tabernacle Walls

Collect

Bible, large sheet of butcher paper (large enough to wrap three sides of card table), markers or crayons, card table, tape.

Do

Children color paper to make colorful Tabernacle walls. Wrap the paper around card table and tape to make the Tabernacle. Children sit under the table as you briefly tell the Bible story.

Helping at the Tabernacle

1 Samuel 1:28; 2:11,18-21,26

I do my best to help and obey because I love God.

Talk About

Enrichment Ideas

1. Children use rulers to draw designs on Tabernacle walls before coloring.

2. Children cut shapes from construction paper and use glue sticks to attach shapes to walls of Tabernacle.

☺ Today in our Bible story, we'll hear about a boy named Samuel who helped at the Tabernacle. Samuel swept the floor and polished the candlesticks. The Tabernacle had colorful walls. We can make Tabernacle walls with many colors, too.

☺ Thank you for holding the tape for me while I taped our Tabernacle walls. What are some ways you help at home?

☺ The Tabernacle was a place where people came to worship God. When Samuel helped in the Tabernacle, he showed love for God. How can we help others to show that we love God?

Helping at the Tabernacle

1 Samuel 1:28; 2:11,18-21,26

"Samuel, Samuel," Eli called. "Samuel, it's time to wake up and start a new day at God's Tabernacle," he said.

Eli had a special job at the Tabernacle. He prayed to God for others. And Eli taught people about God. Samuel helped Eli and took care of the Tabernacle.

Sometimes Eli would say, "Today you may polish the candlesticks." Samuel obeyed. He rubbed and rubbed the candlesticks. Samuel rubbed them until they were shiny and bright.

"We will need some firewood from the woodpile," Eli told Samuel. "Please get some more wood." Samuel obeyed Eli. He carried firewood from the woodpile to the Tabernacle.

Eli told Samuel other jobs to do. And Samuel obeyed all Eli said. When all the work was finished, Eli said, "Open the doors to the Tabernacle. Let the people come inside."

Many people came inside to thank God and to sing glad songs to Him. When all the people went home, it was Samuel's job to close the doors.

Every day Samuel grew taller and stronger. And every day Samuel learned more and more about God. Samuel did a good job of helping Eli at the Tabernacle. Samuel obeyed God by doing his best.

Puppet Talk

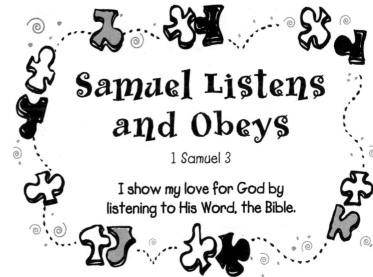

Samuel Listens and Obeys

1 Samuel 3

I show my love for God by listening to His Word, the Bible.

Collect

Bible, construction paper, two Styrofoam cups for each child, markers; optional—yarn, scissors, glue.

Do

1. Children draw Samuel's face on one cup and draw Eli's face on the other. (Optional: Children cut short lengths of yarn and glue onto puppets for hair. Children also glue yarn for a beard for Eli.)

2. Children put their hands inside the cups and use cups as puppets to act out story.

Enrichment Ideas

1. Cut small fabric rectangles. Children glue fabric rectangles onto edge of cups for clothing.

2. Children make puppets using white tube socks. Children draw faces on socks and glue yarn onto socks for hair.

Talk About

☼ Today's Bible story is about a boy named Samuel. One night while Samuel was sleeping, he heard someone call his name three times. Eli told Samuel that it was the Lord talking. Eli told Samuel to say "Speak to me, Lord. I'm listening." Let's make puppets and act out what happened in our Bible story.

☼ Lou, thank you for sharing the markers. God's Word, the Bible, tells us it is good to share. What are some other things you can share?

☼ Samuel listened to God's words. When are some times you can listen to God's words in the Bible?

Samuel Listens and Obeys

1 Samuel 3

Samuel yawned a big yawn and stretched his arms. It was bedtime and Samuel felt very sleepy. After he got himself ready for bed, he lay down and closed his eyes. Then something strange happened! Just as Samuel was going to sleep, he heard someone call, "Samuel! Samuel!" Samuel sat straight up in his bed! "Eli must be calling me," he said. Samuel jumped out of his bed. He ran to where Eli slept. "Here I am. You called me?" Samuel asked.

Eli looked surprised. "I did not call you," Eli said. "Go back to bed, Samuel." Samuel went to his bed and lay down.

Everything was quiet again. "Samuel! Samuel!" Samuel heard the voice again. Samuel ran to Eli. "Here I am. You called me?" Samuel asked. "No," Eli said. "I did not call you. Now go back to bed." So Samuel went back to his bed and lay down.

A third time Samuel heard the voice. "Samuel! Samuel!" And once again he ran to Eli. "Here I am. You called me?" Samuel asked. Then Eli knew God was calling Samuel.

"When you hear the voice again," Eli told Samuel, "say 'Speak to me, God. I am listening.'" Samuel went back to his bed and lay down.

Soon Samuel heard the voice again, "Samuel! Samuel!" Samuel said, "Speak to me, God. I am listening." Then something wonderful happened. God spoke to Samuel. God told Samuel how to obey Him. And Samuel listened carefully to all God told him. Samuel was glad he obeyed Eli. Samuel loved God.

Oil Pictures

Samuel Obeys God

1 Samuel 16:1-13

I obey God because I love Him.

Collect

Bible, newspaper, mineral or cooking oil, pie tins or jar lids, white paper, crayons, cotton balls.

Prepare

Cover table with newspaper. Pour a small amount of oil into pie tins or jar lids.

Do

Children use crayons to color papers. When children are finished coloring, children place pictures facedown on newspaper and use cotton balls to rub a small amount of oil over the backs of their pictures. After papers are dry, children hold papers up to the light to see how the oil changed the pictures.

Enrichment Ideas

1. Instead of pictures, children color people shapes you cut from paper. After children are done coloring, write "I can obey God" on each person shape. Invite children to rub oil lightly on the back of their person shape to create shiny people.

2. For a different look, children paint pictures using watercolors. When paintings are dry, children rub oil on the back of their watercolor pictures. Allow pictures to dry thoroughly.

Talk About

☼ In our Bible story today, God told Samuel to find the new king He had chosen. Samuel obeyed God. Samuel put oil on David's head to show that David would be the new king. We are using oil, too. We are using oil to make our pictures look different.

☼ Carlos, I see that you are sharing your crayons with Ashlyn. You are obeying God. Thank you. What are some other things you can share?

☼ Samuel loved God, so he obeyed everything God told him to do. We can obey God and do what is right, too. What are some ways we can do what is right?

Samuel Obeys God

1 Samuel 16:1-13

Our Bible tells about a boy named Samuel who grew up to be a leader of God's people. Samuel loved and obeyed God. Samuel did what was right and good.

One day God said to Samuel, "I have chosen a new leader, a king, for My people. I want you to show the people their new king. Find a man named Jesse. I have chosen one of Jesse's sons to be the new king. When you get to Bethlehem, I will show you which son I have chosen."

So Samuel obeyed God. Step-step-step. Samuel went to Bethlehem. There he talked to Jesse. Samuel looked at Jesse's sons. The oldest one was tall and strong. *Surely this is the one God wants to be king,* Samuel thought. But God said, "No, he is not the one. The one I have chosen loves Me very much." One, two, three, four, five, six, seven sons walked by Samuel. Each time God said "No, I have not chosen this one to be king." *Who could the king be?* wondered Samuel.

Samuel asked Jesse, "Do you have any more sons?"

"I have one more son," Jesse answered. "David is his name. He is out in the hills, taking care of our sheep."

"Tell David to come here to me," Samuel said. Soon David walked in. David loved God very much. Samuel looked at David. Then God said, "This is the one I have chosen to be the new king." God knew that David loved Him. Samuel loved God, too, and had obeyed God by doing what God had told him to do.

Sheep Masks

Collect

Bible, white paper plates, markers, glue, cotton balls.

Do

Children draw eyes, nose and mouths on plates and glue cotton balls to them to make sheep faces. Children hold up plates in front of their faces as masks.

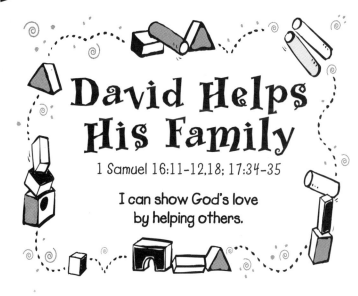

David Helps His Family

1 Samuel 16:11-12,18; 17:34-35

I can show God's love by helping others.

Talk About

☺ Our Bible story tells about a boy named David. David helped his family take care of their sheep. Let's make some sheep masks.

☺ Tony, in Bible times, sheep followed their shepherd to find grass and water. What does a sheep say? Where do you think sheep go to get a drink?

☺ David showed God's love by helping his family by taking care of the sheep. How can you help your family?

Enrichment Ideas

1. Instead of cotton balls, give children small pieces of white wool fabric to glue onto their sheep masks.

2. Shepherds usually name their sheep. Let's name our sheep. How many different names beginning with the letter S can you think of? Repeat with other letters as time permits. On backs of masks, write names children choose.

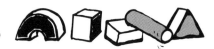

David Helps His Family

1 Samuel 16:11-12,18; 17:34-35

The Bible tells about a boy named David. One day David's father said, "David, you are old enough to do an important job. You are old enough to take care of our sheep." David felt happy! He was glad to be a helper with the sheep

His father said, "You are old enough to find grass for our sheep to eat. You are old enough to find water for them to drink. And you are old enough to bring them safely home at night."

"I will take good care of our sheep," David said.

David worked hard taking care of the sheep. He listened carefully to the sheep. "Baa! Baa! Baa!" the sheep said. David knew they were thirsty. Step, step, step—David walked to find cool water for the sheep to drink. "Baa! Baa! Baa!" the sheep said. David knew the sheep were hungry. Step, step, step—David walked to find a place where green grass grew for the sheep to eat.

While the sheep rested, David often played his harp and sang happy songs about God.

One day David saw a lion creeping toward the sheep. The lion grabbed one of the sheep in its mouth. David jumped up and chased the lion. David caught the lion and pulled the sheep out of its mouth. Gently David patted the sheep and took it back to the other sheep.

David loved God. David was glad to be a good helper for his family.

Picnic Baskets

Collect

Bible, markers, paper lunch bags, scissors, ruler, stapler; optional—magazines or grocery-store advertisements.

Prepare

Draw cut line on lunch bags (see sketch a), marking one bag for each child. (Optional: Cut out pictures of food from magazines or grocery-store advertisements.)

Do

Children cut bags along cut line. Keeping bags flat, children use markers to decorate bags. As children work, cut a strip 1-inch (2.5-cm) wide from the cutoff portions of the bags. When children finish decorating bags, staple strips to bags to form handles for picnic baskets (see sketch b). (Optional: Children choose two or three food pictures to put in their picnic baskets.)

Enrichment Ideas

1. Place bite-size snacks in each child's picnic basket.

2. Provide a large sheet of butcher paper. After children complete their picnic baskets, they cut fringe along all sides of butcher paper and decorate to create a picnic blanket. Children place baskets on blanket for picnic.

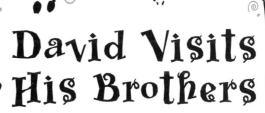

David Visits His Brothers

1 Samuel 17:12-20

Helping the people in my family is a way to show God's love.

Talk About

☺ In our Bible story, David helped his family by bringing food to his brothers. Let's make pretend picnic baskets and have a pretend picnic.

☺ Jody, what are some of your favorite foods? What do you like to eat on a picnic? When you are at a picnic, what is one way to help someone?

☺ At my house, I help my family by mowing the lawn. Helping my family is a way to show God's love. What can you do to help your family and show God's love?

a.

cut

b.

David Visits His Brothers

1 Samuel 17:12-20

Every day David found green grass for his family's sheep. Every day David found cool water for them to drink. Every day David took good care of the sheep. And every day, David's father thought about his seven older sons who were in the army. *What are they doing? Do they have enough to eat?* he must have wondered.

One day David's father said to David, "David, you are old enough to go on a trip by yourself. Please go to see your brothers who are in the army. I want to know how they are doing. I can't go see them." David listened carefully. His father said, "Take them some bread and cheese and corn."

David made plans right away. David probably found another boy to take care of his family's sheep. Then early the next morning, David packed bread and cheese and corn in sacks. Very carefully he loaded the sacks on his donkey. "Good-bye, David," his father called as David walked down the road. "Be careful."

"I'll be careful," David said. "Good-bye!" Clippety-clop, clippety-clop went the donkey's feet on the rocky road.

After a while David saw the tents of the army camp. Then he saw his brothers. David ran to meet his brothers. "I brought you some food from home," David told them. The brothers must have been very glad to get the food. David was glad he could help his father by bringing food to his brothers. David was a good helper. David showed God's love.

Friendship Bracelets

Collect

Bible, straws, ruler, scissors, beads, chenille wires.

Prepare

Cut straws into 1-inch (2.5-cm) pieces. Make a sample bracelet.

Do

Children thread beads and straw pieces onto chenille wires. Place one decorated wire around child's wrist and twist ends to make a bracelet. Each child makes one bracelet to keep and one to give to a friend.

David and Jonathan Are Kind

1 Samuel 16:15-23; 18:1-4; 19:1-7

Being kind to my friends shows God's love.

Talk About

☼ In our Bible story today, David and Jonathan were good friends. Jonathan gave gifts to David. Let's make some friendship bracelets to give to our friends.

☼ When you and a friend want to use the same bead, how can you be kind?

☼ We can show God's love to our friends by being kind to them. What are the names of some of your friends? What can you do to show God's love and be kind to your friends?

Enrichment Ideas

1. Children cut straws themselves.

2. Children thread beads and straws onto chenille wires in a repeating pattern.

3. Children thread colored macaroni and circle-shaped cereal onto bracelets. (Children can eat leftover cereal.)

David and Jonathan Are Kind

1 Samuel 16:15-23; 18:1-4; 19:1-7

King Saul felt grumpy and sad. King Saul felt so grumpy and sad that everyone tried to think of a way to make him feel happy. One of the king's helpers had an idea. "King Saul," the helper said, "if someone could play happy music on the harp, you might feel happy." King Saul thought that was a good idea!

The helper said, "David plays the harp very well. God is with him."

A helper went to talk to David's father. Step-step-step. David was taking care of his family's sheep. But his father said he could go help the king.

Soon David came to live in the king's house. David loved God and was glad to help King Saul by playing his harp. David's music helped King Saul feel happy again.

David liked living in the king's house. One of the people David liked best in the king's house was King Saul's son. His name was Jonathan. David and Jonathan became best friends. They made a special promise to each other. "We will ALWAYS be good friends!" they said. "We will ALWAYS help each other."

One day Jonathan did something to show how much he liked David. "David, I am giving you my coat," Jonathan said. Then Jonathan brought his best bow and arrow to David. "You may have my bow and arrow, too," Jonathan said.

David knew that Jonathan was his good friend. And Jonathan knew David was his good friend. David and Jonathan showed God's love and were kind to each other.

Night Scene

Collect

Bible, 5-foot (1.5-m) square of butcher paper, marker, construction paper (dark blue, green, brown and yellow), glue.

Prepare

On butcher paper, outline an outdoor scene (see sketch a).

Do

Children tear construction paper into pieces. Then children put dots of glue on butcher paper and press torn paper pieces onto the glue (blue pieces on sky, green pieces on trees and brown pieces on hills). Children fill outline of scene and then add yellow paper pieces for stars and a moon (see sketch b).

David and Saul

1 Samuel 26

God helps me show His love, even when it's hard to be kind.

Talk About

☀ Our Bible story today is about King Saul and David. King Saul was trying to hurt David! One night David found King Saul's camp. King Saul was asleep. David could have hurt King Saul, but he didn't. David was kind, even when King Saul was unkind. Let's make a nighttime picture to remind us of the time David was kind.

☀ Kari Beth, Dallas needs some blue paper. How can you help him? Thank you for being kind.

☀ We can ask God to help us be kind, even when it is hard. What are some times it is hard to be kind?

Enrichment Ideas

1. Give children star stickers to place in the night sky.

2. Children create individual night scenes.

a.

b.

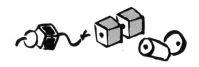

David and Saul

1 Samuel 26

Step, step, step. King Saul and his men looked for David all day. King Saul was angry with David. King Saul wanted to find David and hurt him. Finally, King Saul and his men stopped for the night and set up their camp. King Saul slept on the ground. His men slept all around him.

While King Saul and his men were asleep, David and his men found King Saul's camp. Very quietly, David and his friend Abishai (AB-uh-shi) tip-toed up to King Saul.

"Here's our chance," whispered Abishai. "King Saul wants to hurt you. Let's hurt him!"

"No!" whispered David. "That would be wrong. Let's just take his spear and water jug." So David and Abishai picked up the king's spear and water jug.

They quietly ran to the top of a high hill. "Wake up!" David shouted. David held up King Saul's spear and jug. "See what happened while you slept!" King Saul and his men heard the shouting. They looked around and saw that King Saul's spear and jug were gone. "Is that you, David?" King Saul called out.

"Look!" David shouted. "I have your spear. Let one of your men come and get it. I could have hurt you, but I did not."

King Saul was sorry for the way he had treated David. David turned around and walked back to his men. He could have hurt King Saul, but he didn't. David showed love for God by being kind to King Saul.

Kingly Crowns

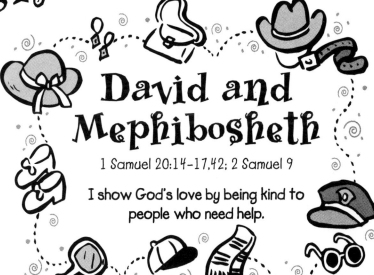

David and Mephibosheth

1 Samuel 20:14-17,42; 2 Samuel 9

I show God's love by being kind to people who need help.

Collect

Bible, 12x18-inch (30.5x45.5-cm) yellow construction paper; ruler; scissors, tape, markers, stapler; optional—yellow Fun Foam, measuring stick, decorative items (sequins, fake jewels, buttons, etc.), glue.

Prepare

Cut paper into 4½x12-inch (11.5x30.5-cm) strips. Tape two strips together for each child (see sketch). (Optional: Cut Fun Foam into 3x18-inch [7.5x45.5-cm] lengths.)

Do

Child draws crown decorations on prepared paper strip. (Optional: Child glues decorative items to Fun Foam strip.) Child tries on crown for size. Staple crown closed. Child wears crown.

Enrichment Ideas

1. Children decorate crowns by drawing jewels in a pattern (e.g., red - blue - green, red - blue - green, etc.).

2. Provide glittery gel pens for children to use to decorate their crowns.

Talk About

☺ Our Bible story today is about a king named David. King David was kind to someone who needed help. Let's make some crowns to help us remember to be kind like King David.

☺ Tracy, thank you for handing the scissors to Luis. You are very kind. What other things can you do to be kind to a friend?

☺ King David showed God's love and helped someone who couldn't walk. When might someone in our class need help?

David and Mephibosheth

1 Samuel 20:14-17,42; 2 Samuel 9

When David became the king, he tried to do good because he loved God. One day, King David remembered his good friend Jonathan, who was dead. They had promised always to help each other and to help each other's children.

How can I help Jonathan now? King David thought. *Maybe there is someone from his family that I could help.*

"Is anyone from Jonathan's family still living?" King David asked his helper.

"There is only one person still alive," the helper said. "He is Jonathan's son, Mephibosheth (mih-FIHB-eh-shehth). His feet are hurt, and he cannot walk very well."

"Bring Mephibosheth to see me right away," King David said. Soon the helper brought Mephibosheth. He walked very slowly toward King David. Mephibosheth felt afraid.

"Oh, Mephibosheth, don't be afraid," King David said. "I promised your father that I would help his children. I want to do as I promised. I want to help you."

Mephibosheth was surprised. "Oh, thank you," Mephibosheth said.

King David said, "I want you to come and live with me. I will give you good food to eat. I will give you nice clothes to wear." So Mephibosheth lived with King David. King David was kind and showed God's love.

Paper-Plate Birds

Collect

Bible, one white paper plate for each child, markers, scissors.

Do

Children fold paper plates in half. Children draw and color face and feathers (see sketch a). Cut as shown. Bend out feathers and bend down tail (see sketch b).

Birds Feed Elijah

1 Kings 17:1-6

God loves and cares for me all the time.

Talk About

☺ In our Bible story, God showed love to a man named Elijah. God sent birds to carry food to Elijah every morning and every night. Let's make some birds today.

☺ Jonas, where do you go in the morning? God cares for you when you go to your grandma's house. Where else do you like to go? God always cares for you.

☺ Every day God is good to us by helping us have food to eat. Logan, what is your favorite meal: breakfast, lunch or dinner?

Enrichment Ideas

1. To make colorful feathers, while paper plate is still flat, children use glue sticks, to glue colored tissue-paper squares to plates.

2. Children glue or tape colorful craft feathers to paper plates.

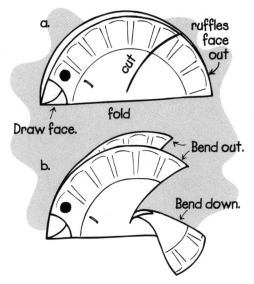

a. ruffles face out

cut

Draw face.

fold

b. Bend out.

Bend down.

Birds Feed Elijah

1 Kings 17:1-6

One day God gave His helper Elijah a very important message. "There will be no rain for a long, long time," God said. *If there is no rain,* Elijah thought, *I'll have nothing to drink. And no food can grow, so I'll have nothing to eat!*

"I will take care of you," God said to Elijah. "I have a special place for you to live. This special place is by a little stream of water. I will send food to you."

Elijah began the long walk to the place where God had told him to go. Step-step-step. Elijah walked down hills. Elijah walked up hills. Tap, tap, tap went his strong walking stick on the rocky path. Finally, Elijah came to the place by the little stream.

Elijah was very tired. He drank the cool water from the stream. He felt better! Elijah sat down by the stream and looked around. Not far away, all the plants were dry and brown. There was no food growing here. There were no people. There were no houses. There weren't even any stores where Elijah could buy food.

What am I going to eat? Elijah thought. Then he remembered, *God said He would take care of me. And God always does what He says.*

Elijah waited by the stream. Soon he saw birds—big black birds—flying toward him. They flew nearer and nearer and nearer. *The birds are holding something,* Elijah thought.

As the birds flew closer, Elijah saw that some birds carried bread. Other birds carried meat. They brought the food to Elijah! God used birds to bring food to Elijah—God did just what He said He would do. God loved and cared for Elijah.

Play-Dough Bread

Collect

Bible, measuring cup, large mixing bowl, flour, cornstarch, salt, warm water, large spoon; optional—food coloring.

Prepare

Pour 1½ cups flour, 1 cup cornstarch and 1 cup salt into large mixing bowl. (Note: Prepare one bowl of ingredients for each group of five or six children.)

Do

1. Pour 1 cup water into mixing bowl. Children take turns stirring mixture to make play dough. If dough is sticky, dust with additional flour. If dough is stiff, add a little water. (Optional: Add a few drops of food coloring to create colored dough.)

2. Children use play dough to make loaves of bread or other objects of their own choice.

Enrichment Ideas

1. Children measure out the ingredients as well as mix the play dough.

2. Children use a variety of tools (rollers, cookie cutters, plastic knives, etc.) to make shapes from play dough.

God Cares for a Widow

1 Kings 17:7-16

God is with me, even when I am afraid.

Talk About

☼ In our Bible story, a widow was afraid she would not have enough food. God cared for her and provided flour and oil for her to make dough. She used the dough to make bread. Let's make some play dough and use it to make bread shapes.

☼ Madison, where do you like to go? God is always with you. I'm glad God cares for us and is with us.

☼ Raul, when might someone your age feel afraid? God is with you then, too! God is with us when we have bad dreams. God is with us all the time. God cares for us. God cares for everyone!

God Cares for a Widow

1 Kings 17:7-16

There was no rain for a long, LONG time, just as God had said. God told His helper Elijah to stay by a little stream, so he would have water to drink every day. But soon there was not even one drop of water left in the stream. What would Elijah do now?

God told Elijah, "Go to a town. A woman there will give you food and water."

Step-step-step. Elijah walked to the town. When Elijah got to the town, he saw a woman picking up sticks to build a fire. Elijah said, "I'm thirsty. Would you please bring me some water?"

Right away the woman went to get water for Elijah. As she left, Elijah called out, "And please bring me a piece of bread to eat."

"Oh, I'm sorry!" the woman told him. "I have only enough flour and oil to make a little bread for my son and me."

"Don't worry," Elijah said kindly. "God has promised that there will be enough food for us all."

The woman baked the bread for Elijah. Then she went to the jar where she kept her flour. There was still flour in the jar! Then she looked in her oil pitcher. The pitcher still had oil in it! There was enough flour and oil to make the bread they needed for dinner. And every day after that, there was enough flour and oil so that the woman could bake more bread. The jar of flour and the pitcher of oil NEVER became empty.

How glad the woman and her son were! God helped Elijah, the woman and her son to have food. God was with the woman, even when she was afraid she would not have enough food.

Plenty of Room

Collect

Bible, large sheet of butcher paper, markers.

Prepare

On large sheet of butcher paper, draw a cutaway view of a large house. Draw at least one room for each child.

Do

Children each choose a room to decorate and identify the room aloud. Encourage children to draw a variety of rooms in the house (bedrooms, kitchen, living room, etc.). Children draw people and objects that might go in the room. If time permits, children decorate more than one room. Display finished mural in classroom or hallway.

Enrichment Ideas

1. Children use carpet, fabric and wallpaper pieces to add decorations to their rooms.

2. From magazines and catalogs, cut pictures of a variety of objects and people that might go in different rooms of a house. Instead of drawing pictures, children glue magazine pictures to the rooms.

Elisha's New Room

2 Kings 4:8-10

God cares for me and gives me what I need.

Talk About

☺ In today's Bible story, a man named Elisha traveled from town to town. He told people messages from God. In one town a man and his wife built a room onto their house for Elisha. Let's decorate the rooms of a house with different things people need.

☺ Pat, you are putting pretty curtains in this bedroom. What does your bedroom at home have in it? God cares for you and gives you what you need.

☺ Jerry, I see you are drawing a kitchen. What is in the kitchen? We keep some of our food in the refrigerator. God helps us have good food to eat. What is your favorite food to eat?

Elisha's New Room

2 Kings 4:8-10

Elisha was a man who went many places to tell people about God. He told people that God loved them. Because Elisha was always traveling, he didn't live in one place.

A kind woman lived in one town Elisha visited. While Elisha was there, she listened to him talk about God. She knew Elisha loved God. She thought, *Poor Elisha. He travels from town to town without a place to stay. Maybe he would like to eat with me and my husband today.* "Elisha," the woman asked, "would you like to eat dinner with my husband and me?"

"Yes, thank you," Elisha answered. They ate a good-tasting meal together. Elisha went to many other places to tell more people about God. But whenever he came to this town, he ate dinner with the kind woman and her husband.

One day the woman said to her husband, "I want to do something kind for Elisha. Let's build a room on the roof of our house for him. We can put a chair, table, lamp and bed in the room. When Elisha comes to visit, he can eat with us and sleep in his own room."

The woman's husband thought it was a good idea, so they began to build a room for Elisha. Zip, zip, zip went the saw. Pound, pound, pound went the hammer. They worked and worked building the room. Finally, Elisha's room was ready. The woman put the chair, table, lamp and bed in the room. The room was just right!

When Elisha came to town, the woman said, "Come quickly. We have something special to show you." The woman and her husband walked with Elisha up the stairs to his new room. Elisha must have been surprised. Now he could sleep in his very own room! Elisha was very glad God cared for him and gave him kind friends.

Sad and Happy Naaman

Collect

Bible, construction paper, crayons or markers.

Prepare

For each child, draw one person shape on a sheet of construction paper and cut out.

Do

Children draw sad face on one side of person and happy face on the other. Children make sores by marking dot shapes on the sad-face side of shape. Children color happy-face side. Children first show sad face and then happy face.

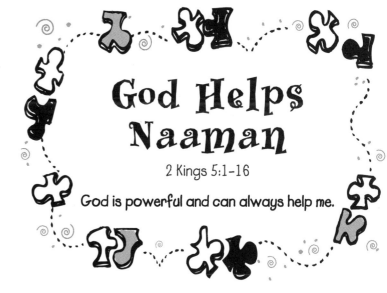

God Helps Naaman

2 Kings 5:1-16

God is powerful and can always help me.

Enrichment Ideas

1. Children use dot stickers to make sores.

2. Children squeeze glue drops onto Naaman's body on the sad-face side. Children sprinkle glitter on glue drops to make sores.

Talk About

☺ In today's Bible story, a man named Naaman was very sick. Naaman was sad. When Naaman obeyed God, God made him well. Then Naaman was very happy. You can each make a happy and sad Naaman.

☺ God is so powerful that He can always help us. When we're sick, God helps us. Elena, who did God give you to take care of you when you are sick?

☺ I'm glad that God helps me by listening to me when I pray. Shana, when do you pray to God? God hears your prayers. God is great and will always help you.

God Helps Naaman

2 Kings 5:1-16

A man named Naaman had a terrible problem: He had a sickness called leprosy. The sickness made painful sores on Naaman's skin. Naaman knew he would get sicker and sicker. He might even die! His family must have been very sad.

Naaman's wife had a servant girl. This girl was from the country of Israel. She knew that in Israel there was a man named Elisha who loved God. God helped Elisha do amazing things. The servant girl said, "I wish Naaman would go to see Elisha." The girl thought Elisha might be able to help Naaman.

Right away Naaman's wife told Naaman the news about Elisha. Naaman decided to go see Elisha. The king of Naaman's country wrote a letter to the king of Israel. Naaman took the letter. He also took gifts of silver, gold and clothing. Naaman went to the king of Israel. The king read the letter: "Here is Naaman. I want you to make his sickness go away."

But the king said, "I'm not God! I can't make Naaman well!"

Soon, Elisha heard about Naaman's visit. Elisha asked the king to send Naaman to him. Naaman came to Elisha's door. Elisha's servant talked to Naaman. "Go and wash yourself seven times in the Jordan River," the servant said. "Then you will be well."

At first Naaman didn't want to wash in the Jordan River. It was too muddy! But then Naaman changed his mind. He walked to the river. He waded in. He ducked under the water one, two, three, four, five, six, seven times. He wiped the water from his eyes. He looked at his skin. The sores were gone! Naaman was all well! Naaman said, "Now I know there is only one God—the one true God!" Naaman knew God was powerful and could help him.

Building Rubbings

Joash Repairs the Temple

2 Kings 12:4-15; 2 Chronicles 24:1-14

I can learn from others ways to obey God.

Collect

Bible, construction paper, building materials (shingle, wood, carpet, linoleum, tile, etc.), unwrapped crayons.

Do

Give each child a sheet of construction paper. Child places paper on top of one of the building material items. Child colors over the top of item with the side of an unwrapped crayon until texture shows on paper. Child repeats activity with other items.

Talk About

❂ In our Bible story today, King Joash asked people to help fix the Temple. Helpers swept and cleaned and fixed up the Temple, so people could worship God again. Today we are going to make rubbings of things people use in building.

❂ King Joash helped God's people learn ways to obey God. We can learn ways to obey God, too. Let's thank God for people who teach us to obey Him.

❂ Russell, who teaches you about the Bible at home? What is a way your brother told you to obey God?

Enrichment Ideas

1. Instead of rubbing, children trace around items on paper and color inside the outline.

2. Provide a variety of toy tools (hammer, screwdriver, etc.) around which children may trace.

Joash Repairs the Temple

2 Kings 12:4-15; 2 Chronicles 24:1-14

God's people were glad for their beautiful Temple. (The Temple was a special place where people went to pray and learn about God.) The people brought gifts of money to the Temple. The helpers in the Temple kept it clean and beautiful. They swept the floors. They dusted the furniture. They rubbed the bowls and vases until they were bright and shiny.

After a while some of the people stopped coming to the Temple. Then more and MORE people stopped coming to the Temple. Finally, no one visited. No one took care of the Temple for many years.

King Joash was sad because God's Temple looked awful. The walls were broken. Dust and dirt covered everything. King Joash loved God. He wanted God's people to learn ways to love God and obey Him. King Joash thought, *We MUST make God's Temple beautiful again, so people can come to pray and learn about God. But we will need MANY helpers. And we will need LOTS of money!*

King Joash's helpers told God's people, "We need EVERYONE to help make the Temple beautiful again. You may help by bringing money. Put your gifts of money in the big box at the Temple." Mothers and fathers, boys and girls came to drop their money in the big box. Clink! Clink! Clink! They were glad to give their money.

Soon there was enough money to pay helpers to fix the Temple. Zzzzz, zzzzz went their saws. Tap, tap, tap went their hammers. Some helpers dusted the furniture and swept the floor. Some helpers shined the bowls and vases. And some helpers made new bowls and vases. The Temple was clean and beautiful again.

King Joash called God's people to come to pray and learn about God at the Temple. God's people were glad to worship Him again! King Joash helped the people learn ways to obey God.

My Very Own Scroll

Collect

Bible, shelf paper or adding-machine paper, measuring stick, scissors, markers, craft sticks, tape, rubber bands.

Prepare

Cut one 4x18-inch (10x45.5-cm) length of shelf paper or one 18-inch (45.5-cm) length of adding-machine paper for each child.

Do

1. Using markers, children decorate a length of paper.

2. When scrolls are decorated, give two craft sticks to each child. Children tape a craft stick to each end of their scrolls. Rolling from each end, children roll up their scrolls. Children slip rubber bands over scrolls to keep them from unrolling.

Enrichment Ideas

1. Give each child a 4x18-inch (10x45.5-cm) length of brown butcher paper or paper grocery bag. Children crumple and uncrumple paper several times. Children use crumpled paper to make scrolls.

2. On a large sheet of paper, print a Bible verse such as "Love one another" (1 John 4:7). Children copy the words of the verse on their scrolls.

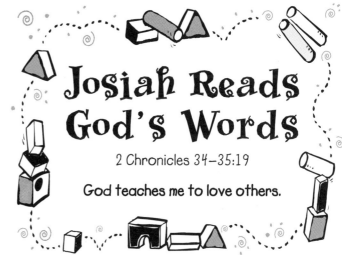

Josiah Reads God's Words

2 Chronicles 34—35:19

God teaches me to love others.

Talk About

☼ In today's Bible story, King Josiah read God's Word to all the people. In Bible times, God's Word was written on a scroll, which is like a long rolled-up sheet of paper. Let's make some scrolls of our own.

☼ God's Word teaches us to love others. Matthew, I saw you hand Kerry a marker. It was kind of you to help her. You know how to show love to others! What are some other ways you can help your friends?

☼ Anna, what is one way someone in your family shows love to you? How can you do what God teaches and show love to someone in your family?

Josiah Reads God's Words

2 Chronicles 34—35:19

For many years, the scroll of God's Words had been lost. God's Temple was broken down and dirty. But young King Josiah loved God. One day he said, "It is time to clean the Temple. We need many helpers to make the Temple clean and beautiful."

Many people came to help. Some helpers swept and scrubbed the Temple. Swish, swish went their brooms. Some helpers fixed broken furniture. Bang, bang went their hammers. While the helpers worked hard, the Temple leader picked up something covered with dust. *What is this?* he wondered. Poof! He blew off the dust. "It's a scroll," he said. (A scroll is like a long rolled-up sheet of paper.) Carefully he unrolled the scroll. He read a few words. Then he told the king's helper, "Here is a scroll with God's words written on it! King Josiah will want to see this!"

The helper ran to the king's house. "Look at this, King Josiah," he said. "The Temple leader found this scroll! It has God's words written on it."

King Josiah listened to one of his helpers read God's words. King Josiah loved God and wanted to obey God's words. He invited all of God's people to come to the Temple. Boys and girls, mothers and fathers, grandmothers and grandfathers came to hear God's words. King Josiah unrolled the Bible scroll and read God's words. The people listened.

King Josiah and the people promised to obey God's words. As long as King Josiah lived, he and the people obeyed God.

Cereal Walls

Collect

Bible, construction paper, glue, square-shaped cereal in several shallow bowls.

Do

Children glue cereal squares onto papers to make walls.

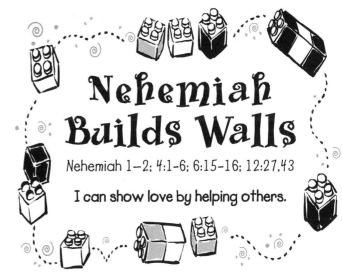

Nehemiah Builds Walls

Nehemiah 1—2; 4:1-6; 6:15-16; 12:27,43

I can show love by helping others.

Talk About

☼ Today in our Bible story, a man named Nehemiah helped God's people rebuild the walls around their city. The walls helped the people stay safe. You can make a picture of a wall. Let's pretend these pieces of cereal are stones. You can glue these stones onto your paper to make a wall.

☼ Sophia, thank you for passing the bowl of cereal so that Catalina can reach it. You are showing love when you help others. What are some other ways you like to help?

☼ The people were glad to help each other rebuild the walls. They showed love to each other when they helped each other. Let's name some other ways we can help people.

Enrichment Ideas

1. Provide construction paper squares and rectangles. Children glue on paper to create walls.

2. Provide cereal in several colors. Children glue cereal to make patterns.

Nehemiah Builds Walls

Nehemiah 1-2; 4:1-6; 6:15-16; 12:27,43

Nehemiah was a special helper to the king. He lived in a country far from his real home. One day, Nehemiah's brother came and told Nehemiah sad news. "The city where we used to live had a strong wall. Now it is broken. The city is not safe."

Nehemiah was sad. So Nehemiah did something very important: He prayed to God. He knew God would hear his prayer.

When the king saw Nehemiah, he asked, "Why are you so sad, my friend?"

Nehemiah said, "I am sad because the wall around my city is broken down. I would like to go and help the people build the wall again."

The king said, "You may go and help the people build the wall. Come back when it is finished." Nehemiah was very happy. He thanked the king and started off to the city.

When Nehemiah came to the city, he said to all the people, "We can build the wall. We can make it strong again. Who will help?"

"My family will help," said a father. "We will cut some stones."

"My family will help," said another father. "We will cut down trees to make the gates."

Bang! Bang! The hammers and chisels cut stone. Zzzzzz! Zzzzzz! The saws cut wood. Fathers and mothers, boys and girls all helped.

For many days, the people worked together. Finally the wall was finished. Everyone was glad that the city was safe again. The people were glad they had shown love and helped each other.

Beautiful Palaces

Collect

Bible, marker, length of butcher paper, metallic wrapping paper, scissors, ruler, glue, crayons; optional—glitter crayons.

Prepare

Draw a large palace outline on butcher paper (see sketch). Cut wrapping paper into 2-inch (5-cm) squares.

Do

Children decorate palace by gluing wrapping-paper squares to palace outline and coloring palace with crayons. (Optional: Children use glitter crayons.)

Esther Is Brave

Esther 2—9

God helps me do good things.

Enrichment Ideas

1. Cut windows and doors in a large box. Children decorate box to create a palace.

2. Children paint palace walls using gold and silver paint.

Talk About

☼ In our Bible story today, Queen Esther did a good thing by helping God's people when they were in danger. Queen Esther talked to the king about a way to save God's people. Queen Esther lived in a palace. Let's pretend we're decorating a beautiful palace.

☼ You are helping Amy color the palace, Yolanda. Thank you. Helping others is a good thing to do. What are some other ways to help others?

☼ God helps us do good things. Samy, what good things can you do at your house? God will help you take turns with your brother.

Esther Is Brave

Esther 2—9

A young woman named Esther and her cousin Mordecai were Jews who lived in a country far from Israel. (God's people were called Jews.) Mordecai was kind to Esther and cared for her. One day, King Xerxes (ZUHRK-sees) chose Esther to be his new queen!

The king had a helper named Haman. Haman hated Mordecai so much that he wanted to kill him. Because Mordecai was a Jew, Haman wanted to kill all Jews. Haman tricked the king into making a law to kill all the Jews.

Now Esther had a big problem. Haman and King Xerxes did not know that she was a Jew. She wanted to talk to the king about Haman's plans, but she was afraid. Anyone who talked to the king without being invited could be killed—even the queen.

Esther said, "I will go to the king, even though I am afraid." For three days, Esther, Mordecai and all the other Jews prayed and did not eat anything. Then Esther got dressed up. She stood at the door where the king was. When she walked through the door, she wondered what the king would do. When King Xerxes saw her, he SMILED! Esther came up to the king.

Esther asked the king and Haman to eat dinner with her. Haman was very HAPPY to be the only person invited to have dinner with the king and queen! So King Xerxes and Haman came to Esther's dinner. Esther told the king that someone was going to KILL all of her people. She asked the king to please save her life and the lives of all her people. The king asked, "Who would DO such a thing?"

Esther pointed at Haman. "The man who wants to do this is HAMAN!"

King Xerxes had Haman taken away! Then the king wrote a new law to protect the Jews. God had helped Queen Esther do good!

Writing Fun

Collect

Bible, a variety of items used for writing or drawing (pencils, markers, crayons, etc.), alphabet stencils, paper.

Do

Children experiment writing or drawing with a variety of items. Children use stencils to trace letters.

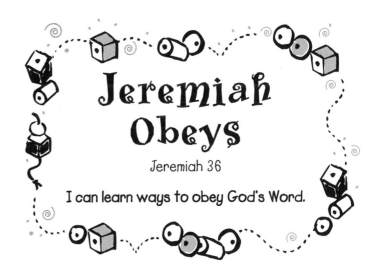

Jeremiah Obeys

Jeremiah 36

I can learn ways to obey God's Word.

Talk About

☼ In our Bible story, Jeremiah and his helper, Baruch (buh-ROOK), obeyed God. Baruch helped Jeremiah write God's Word. God's Word is the Bible. Let's write some letters today.

☼ When we learn about Bible stories and verses, we learn ways to obey God. Diego, when do you hear Bible stories and verses?

☼ Taking turns is a good way to obey God's Word. Let's name some times that we can take turns.

Enrichment Ideas

1. Give each child a sheet of paper and an envelope. Invite children to write pretend letters or draw pictures to give to others. Help children fold and put letters or drawings into envelopes.

2. Children cut words or letters from magazines and glue them onto paper to create word collages. Help interested children identify letters and/or words.

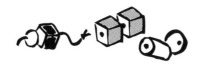

Jeremiah Obeys

Jeremiah 36

Jeremiah told the people to love and obey God. But the people were not obeying God. God still loved the people. He wanted them to stop doing what was wrong. God told Jeremiah to write down God's very important words.

Jeremiah called his helper Baruch (buh-ROOK). Jeremiah said the messages from God out loud. Baruch wrote the messages down on a scroll. (A scroll is like a long rolled-up sheet of paper.)

"Take the scroll to the Temple and read it to the people," Jeremiah told Baruch. (The Temple was the place where God's people came to pray and learn about God.)

Baruch took the scroll to God's Temple. He read it in a loud, clear voice. Some people went to King Jehoiakim (juh-HOY-uh-kuhm) and told him about the scroll.

The king ordered one of his helpers to bring the scroll to him. One of the king's helpers read it to him. The king was angry about what God's words said! The king grabbed a knife. He cut the scroll apart. He burned each piece in the fire!

The king may have thought he had gotten rid of God's words. But God told Jeremiah, "Write the scroll again." Jeremiah and Baruch obeyed God. They wrote another scroll just like the first one. Baruch read the scroll to the people again. Even though the king was angry, Jeremiah obeyed God by helping others learn about God's Word.

Veggie Place Mats

Collect

Bible, one or more kinds of vegetables (bell peppers, celery, carrots, potatoes, etc.), knife, washable-ink pads, construction paper; optional—clear Con-Tact paper.

Prepare

Cut vegetables into chunks large enough for children to handle easily.

Do

Using cut vegetables and washable-ink pads, children make prints on sheets of construction paper. (Optional: After prints dry, cover decorated construction paper with clear Con-Tact paper.)

Enrichment Ideas

1. On a large sheet of paper, print "Love the Lord your God." Children use markers to copy the words onto their place mats before decorating them.

2. Provide a variety of stickers for children to add to their place mats.

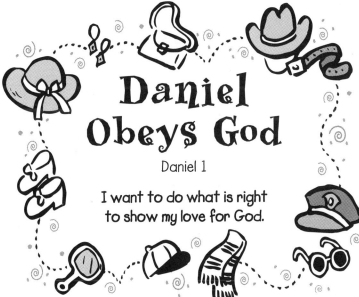

Daniel Obeys God

Daniel 1

I want to do what is right to show my love for God.

Talk About

☼ In our Bible story, Daniel and his friends loved and obeyed God. They ate only the foods God had said to eat. They ate vegetables. Let's use some vegetables to decorate place mats.

☼ Leo, you moved over to give Rosalinda room to work. You did what was right by being kind! What are some ways that you can be kind at home?

☼ Daniel and his friends did what was right by obeying God. We can show our love for God by doing what is right, too. What are some ways you can do what is right?

Daniel Obeys God

Daniel 1

King Nebuchadnezzar (nehb-uh-kuhd-NEHZ-uhr) went to Israel with a strong army. His army took many people from Israel back to their country, Babylon. Four boys were among the people taken from Israel. One of the boys was named Daniel. Daniel and his three friends walked for days and days until, finally, they came to Babylon.

When they got to Babylon, a helper of the king came to choose servants for the king. The helper chose the strongest, healthiest and smartest young men. Daniel and his three friends were chosen! As the king's servants, Daniel and his friends would go to a special school. They would learn to speak and read the king's language. They were also supposed to eat food right from the king's table—the same food the king ate!

The king's food looked and smelled very good. But God had told His people not to eat certain foods. And the king's food was not something they could eat. Daniel and his friends decided to obey God's rules.

Daniel and his friends talked to the guard who was in charge of meals. Daniel asked the guard to give them a test: For 10 days, the boys would eat only vegetables and drink only water. Then they would see if this was a good idea. The guard agreed!

For 10 days, Daniel and his three friends ate only vegetables and drank only water. Then the guard looked at the four boys. Daniel and his friends looked better and stronger than the others did! So the guard let them keep on eating the way they were supposed to. They were able to do what was right and show they loved God!

Gold Collages

Collect

Bible, scissors, gold materials (gold wrapping paper, gold pens, gold tissue paper, etc.), construction paper, glue.

Do

Children cut and glue gold materials onto paper to create collages.

The Fiery Furnace

Daniel 3

I love God and I know He will care for me.

Talk About

☺ In today's Bible story, Daniel's friends would not bow down to pray to a big shiny gold statue. They only wanted to pray to God. Even though the king was angry, Daniel's friends knew God would keep them safe. We are going to make collages from gold materials today.

☺ Tom, you are using your hands to glue gold paper. I'm glad God cares for us by giving us hands. What else can you do with your hands?

☺ Another way that God cares for us is by giving us moms and dads and grandmas and grandpas who help us. Nathan, what does your grandpa do to help you?

Enrichment Ideas

1. Children use gold paint to paint pictures.

2. Before class, spray-paint macaroni noodles, rice, beans, etc. gold. Add these gold items to collage materials.

The Fiery Furnace

Daniel 3

Daniel and his three friends worked for King Nebuchadnezzar of Babylon. One day, the king decided to make a big statue covered with shiny gold. It was a statue of himself. The statue was set up in a place where everyone could come and see it.

The king's messenger told the people, "When the music plays, bow down and pray to this statue. If you do not bow down, you will be thrown in a furnace and be burned up!"

But Daniel's three friends would not pray to the big statue. They would only pray to God! The music began to play. Everyone else bowed down low, but the three friends did not bow down. They stood tall. When King Nebuchadnezzar heard that they had not bowed to his statue, he was angry! The three friends were brought to the king. The king roared, "If you don't bow NOW, you'll be thrown into the furnace!"

The three friends said, "O king, our God is able to save us from the fire." Daniel's three friends loved God and knew He would care for them.

The soldiers tied up the friends. They threw the three men into the middle of the hot flames. Then the king looked in the furnace. He saw the three friends walking in the middle of the hot, hot fire. And there was someone else in there, too. It was an angel God sent to keep the three friends safe.

King Nebuchadnezzar shouted for the men to come out of the fire. When the three friends came out of the furnace, they were not burned at all. They didn't even smell like smoke! God had kept them safe, even in the fire. King Nebuchadnezzar knew God had kept the men safe, so he praised the one true God.

Colorful Letters

Collect

Bible, length of butcher paper, markers or crayons, tape.

Prepare

Print the words "Daniel," "king," "wall," "listen" and "obey" in large block letters on the paper. Tape paper to wall at children's eye level.

Do

Children color in letters as you talk about the Bible story.

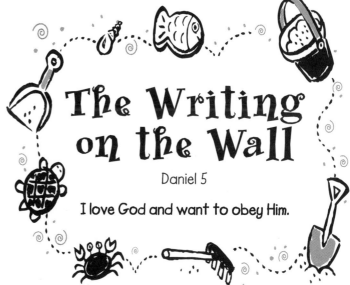

The Writing on the Wall

Daniel 5

I love God and want to obey Him.

Talk About

☀ Today in our Bible story, a king saw words appear on the wall. The words were a special message from God for the king. Daniel obeyed God by telling the king what the words meant. Let's color some words that have been written on the paper on our wall.

☀ Patty, thank you for moving over so that Shayron can write too. When you are kind, you obey God. Name some other times you can be kind.

☀ Daniel obeyed God when he lived in a palace. Sophia, where do you live? You can obey God at your house. When we obey God, it shows we love Him.

Enrichment Ideas

1. Children print their own letters or numbers on the paper as they color.

2. Give children glue sticks and small bits of construction paper to glue inside the letters to create mosaics.

The Writing on the Wall

Daniel 5

King Belshazzar (behl-SHAHZ-uhr), the king of Babylon, liked to have lots of parties. One night, King Belshazzar brought out some beautiful gold cups. The cups had been stolen from God's Temple in Jerusalem. The king did not care that these things belonged to God. King Belshazzar did not love or obey God. He and his friends drank from the gold cups from God's Temple.

Suddenly, something very strange happened. A big hand appeared out of nowhere! The finger of the hand began to write on the wall! King Belshazzar watched the hand. He became very scared! No one could tell what the writing meant. The king asked his wise helpers to look at the writing. None of them knew what the writing meant.

Then the queen told King Belshazzar that Daniel was very wise. Daniel was a man who loved God and obeyed God. The queen told Belshazzar to call for Daniel. The king asked Daniel to tell him what the writing meant. Daniel said that the words meant God had seen the ways King Belshazzar had not obeyed God.

"Now," said Daniel, "God is going to END your time as king. Other people will take your place."

That very same night, God's warning came true. Another king came and took over the city. Daniel was given a new job by the new king! And Daniel continued to show that he loved God and wanted to obey Him.

114

Mane Event

Collect

Bible, paper plates, scissors, hole punch, yarn, measuring stick, markers (brown, yellow and orange), stapler.

Prepare

Cut plates in half. Cut one mane and one set of ears for each child (see sketch a). Punch a hole at each end of the manes. Cut two 18-inch (45.5-cm) lengths of yarn for each child.

Do

1. Using markers, each child colors a mane and two ears. Assist children in cutting slits in the edges of the manes and folding over every other section (see sketch b).

2. Help children place ears on mane and staple in place. Children thread a length of yarn through each hole on their manes. Assist children in tying knots. Children place manes on their heads and tie under their chins (see sketch c).

Enrichment Ideas

1. Cut brown, yellow and orange construction paper into 1x4-inch (2.5x10-cm) strips. Children glue construction-paper strips to add to their manes.

2. Before class, precut pieces of fuzzy fabric. In class, children glue fabric pieces to lion's ears.

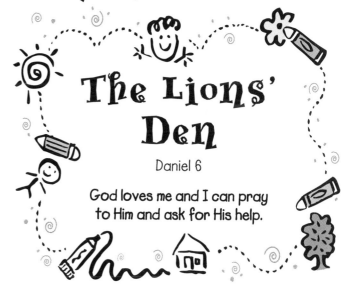

The Lions' Den

Daniel 6

God loves me and I can pray to Him and ask for His help.

Talk About

☼ In our Bible story, Daniel prayed to God. God loved Daniel and kept him safe when he was in a cave filled with lions. Let's make lions' manes to remind us of the way God loved and helped Daniel.

☼ We can pray to God every day. We can thank God for the good things He gives us. Jorge, when is a time you can talk to God? What can you thank Him for?

☼ I like to pray to God when I get up in the morning. Carrie, when is a time you can talk to God?

The Lions' Den

Daniel 6

Daniel loved God. One way he showed his love was by praying to God. Daniel prayed to God one, two, three times every day.

Daniel was the king's most important helper. The king liked Daniel very much. But there were some mean men who did not like Daniel. They were angry that the king liked Daniel. These mean men thought of a plan to get Daniel in trouble with the king. They went to the king and said, "King, we think you should make a rule that everyone must pray only to you. If people pray to anyone else but you, they will be thrown into a cave filled with lions!"

The king thought this rule was a good idea. The king sent helpers to tell all the people they must pray only to him. The angry men watched to see what Daniel would do.

The next day Daniel opened his window, just like he always did. Daniel prayed to God, just like he always did. He did not pray to the king. The mean men watched as Daniel prayed to God. Then the mean men ran to tell the king what they saw.

Daniel was in trouble. The king was sad. The king did not want Daniel to be hurt, but the king had to obey the rule, too. Daniel was put into a big cave where lions lived. All night the king worried about Daniel's safety. The next morning, the king ran to the lions' cave. He called, "Daniel! DANIEL!"

Daniel called back from inside the cave, "King, I am safe. God took care of me!" The king was so glad that Daniel was not hurt! Daniel came out of the cave. The king knew that God had helped Daniel and kept him safe from the lions. Then the king told everyone what God had done. He made a new rule that everyone should love God and pray only to Him. Daniel was glad God loved and helped him.

Paper-Plate Fish

Collect

Bible, markers, paper plates, scissors, stapler.

Prepare

Draw lines on paper plates (see sketch a).

Do

1. Give each child a paper plate. Assist as each child cuts along lines. The opening becomes the fish's mouth. For the tail, staple cutoff portion opposite the mouth.

2. Children use markers to decorate their fish, adding facial features, scales, fins, etc. (see sketch b).

Jonah and the Big Fish

Jonah

I can obey God by showing His love to others.

Talk About

☀ In our Bible story, God told Jonah to go to Nineveh to tell the people an important message. Jonah disobeyed God and tried to go somewhere else! But God sent a storm and a big fish to help Jonah learn to obey. You can make a fish as a reminder of Jonah!

☀ Michelle, thank you for sharing the markers with Estrella. Sharing is a way to show love to others. What are some other things you can share?

☀ One thing God tells us to do is to show His love to others. Gabriel, who is someone you can show love to? Your brother Jaime? What can you do to show love to Jaime?

Enrichment Ideas

1. Thin glue with water in a shallow pan. Children use brushes to apply thinned glue to paper plates. Children place pieces of one or more colors of tissue paper on glue for scales.

2. Children paint or color a length of butcher paper to look like the ocean. Attach completed fish to the ocean.

a. Cut / Cut

b.

Jonah and the Big Fish

Jonah

Jonah told people messages from God. One day, God told Jonah, "Go to Nineveh. Tell the people that they have disobeyed Me."

But Jonah did NOT like the people of Nineveh, so instead of going to Nineveh, Jonah got on a boat that was going the other way! He did not want to obey God. He went down into the bottom of the boat and went to sleep.

God sent a big storm. The waves were crashing. All the sailors were very afraid! But Jonah knew that God had sent the storm because Jonah had disobeyed. Jonah told the sailors, "Throw me into the ocean. Then the storm will stop." One, two, THREE! The soldiers threw Jonah into the water. Sure enough, the waves stopped crashing.

The boat was safe. But Jonah was in the ocean! Then God sent a huge fish. The fish opened its mouth wide and WHOOSH! Jonah was in the belly of the big fish!

Jonah began to pray. He asked God to forgive him. He thanked God for rescuing him, even though he had disobeyed. Jonah prayed and he waited. Then God sent that big fish close to land. The fish began to cough and choke and AACK!—it coughed Jonah right up onto the beach! Then God talked to Jonah again.

God said, "Go! Tell those people they have disobeyed Me!" And this time Jonah obeyed! He went to Nineveh. He told everyone he saw that they had disobeyed God. The people listened. Then they obeyed God. They asked God to forgive them! And God did forgive them.

Angel Ornaments

Collect

Bible, small paper plates, scissors, small paper doilies, ruler, 2-inch (5-cm) circles made from pink construction paper, chenille wires (white, gold and/or metallic), transparent tape, markers.

Prepare

Cut paper plates and doilies in half, one half of each for each child. Cut chenille wires into 6-inch (15-cm) lengths.

Do

1. Children bring the corners of the cut edge of each paper plate half together to a create cone shape for angel body. Help children tape edges together. Children tape a paper doily half to the back of each cone to make wings.

2. Children use markers to draw a face on each pink circle and tape face to an angel. Help children make halos from chenille wire: form a loop with a stem; tape stem to back of angel face.

Enrichment Ideas

1. Older children cut paper plates and doilies in half and trace and cut out face circles.

2. Children decorate angel bodies with seasonal stickers.

Mary Hears Good News

Matthew 1:18-25; Luke 1:26-56

I can thank God for His promise to send His Son, Jesus.

Talk About

☼ In today's Bible story, an angel talked to Mary and then later to Joseph. The angel told good news: God's Son, Jesus, would be born. Let's make some angel ornaments to remind us of the good news about Jesus.

☼ We can thank God for His promise to send Jesus to be born. At Chistmastime, whose birth do we celebrate? I'm glad God kept His promise and sent Jesus to be born.

☼ Olivia, what does your family do to celebrate Jesus' birth? Let's thank God for His promise to send Jesus to be born.

Mary Hears Good News

Matthew 1:18-25; Luke 1:26-56

A long, long time ago, God promised He would send His special Son. God's people waited and waited and waited. They wanted God to send His Son. One person who waited for God's promise was a young woman named Mary.

One day Mary was alone. She looked up. Standing right there beside her was an angel! Mary had never seen an angel before!

"Hello, Mary," the angel said. "God is with you." Mary was surprised and afraid. "Don't be afraid, Mary," the angel said. "God loves you. He has chosen you to be the mother of a very special baby. You will name the baby Jesus. He will be very great. This special baby will be God's own Son!" Mary was glad to hear this promise!

How exciting! Mary hurried to tell her cousin Elizabeth the wonderful news. Mary walked into Elizabeth's house. Just then God let Elizabeth know that Mary was going to be the mother of His Son, Jesus. Elizabeth said, "Mary, you're a special woman and your baby is very special!" Mary was glad. She thanked God. She told God she loved Him.

Very soon a man named Joseph was going to be Mary's husband. One night Joseph was asleep. An angel talked to him in a dream. "Mary is going to have a special baby. He is God's Son," the angel said. "You will name Him Jesus." Joseph was glad God was sending His Son, Jesus. Joseph was glad he could help care for this special baby God had promised.

Surprise Names

Collect

Bible, white paper, white crayon or candle, pencil, newspaper or plastic tablecloth, cups of water, paintbrushes, watercolors.

Prepare

For each child, use white crayon or bottom of candle to firmly print child's name on a sheet of paper (make thick lines with lots of wax). Use pencil to write child's name on the back of the paper.

Do

Cover table with newspaper or tablecloth. Place cups of water on table for children to dip brushes in while painting. Children paint over papers with watercolors to reveal their names.

Enrichment Ideas

1. After paint is dry, children use glue to outline their name and then sprinkle glitter along lines of glue.

2. With white crayons, children draw pictures or designs of their own choosing. Children paint on paper to reveal pictures.

John Is Born

Luke 1:5-25,57-80

I'm glad God loves everyone in the world.

Talk About

☼ In our Bible story today, a man named Zechariah could not talk. Zechariah wrote his son's name for people to see. Let's have some fun finding our names.

☼ Janey, what color do you want to use? You can find your name by painting on the paper. God loves you!

☼ When Zechariah's son John grew up, he told people about God's love. God loves everyone in the world. What is the name of one of your friends? God loves you and your friend.

John Is Born

Luke 1:5-25,57-80

Zechariah and his wife, Elizabeth, loved God. They were old. They had no children. One day, Zechariah was working in the Temple. He looked up. He saw an angel! He was surprised and afraid!

The angel said, "Don't be afraid! You and Elizabeth will have a baby! This baby will make you glad! You will name this baby John. This baby will grow up and do an important job. He will help people get ready for Jesus!"

Zechariah didn't believe the angel. He asked, "How can I be sure this is true?"

The angel said, "I have been sent from God to tell you this good news! Because you did not believe me, you will not be able to talk until your son is born!"

The angel left. Zechariah walked outside. People could see he was excited! But he couldn't talk!

After a time, Zechariah and Elizabeth's baby was born. Friends and relatives came to see him! They wanted to name the baby Zechariah, just like the baby's father. But Elizabeth said, "No! His name is John!"

The relatives and friends were surprised. They asked Zechariah what the baby's name should be. Zechariah wrote "His name is John." Suddenly, he could talk!

Zechariah prayed and thanked God! Zechariah told about John's very important job. When John grew up, he was going to help people get ready for Jesus. John was going to tell the people about God's love and promises!

Manger Pictures

Collect

Bible, construction paper, craft sticks, glue, short lengths of yellow yarn; optional—straw or raffia.

Prepare

Make a sample manger picture.

Do

Children glue craft sticks and yellow yarn onto paper to make manger pictures. (Optional: Use straw or raffia instead of yarn.)

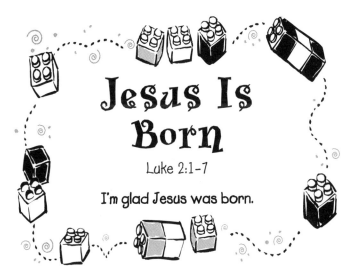

Jesus Is Born

Luke 2:1-7

I'm glad Jesus was born.

Enrichment Ideas

1. Children draw animals (cows, sheep, donkeys, goats, etc.) around the manger.

2. Children place several animal stickers around their manger scene.

Talk About

☸ Today in our Bible story, Jesus was born in the town of Bethlehem. He slept in a manger. A manger is a box where food is put for animals to eat. We are going to make manger pictures.

☸ Bart, how many animals will eat from your manger? What kind of food will your animals eat?

☸ When it was time for Jesus to be born, Mary and Joseph couldn't find a house to stay in. They stayed in a stable. A stable is a place where animals live. What animals might have been in the stable where Jesus was born? I'm glad Jesus was born.

Jesus Is Born

Luke 2:1-7

One day Joseph said to Mary, "We must go to Bethlehem. We must write our names in the king's book." So Joseph and Mary began to pack for their trip. After all their things were packed, they started to go to Bethlehem.

Mary probably rode on a donkey. Clippety-clop, clippety-clop, clippety-clop went the donkey's feet against the rocks on the road. Joseph walked beside her. It was a long, hard, bumpy ride for Mary. It was almost time for Mary to have a baby. Mary and Joseph knew that this baby would be very, very special. This baby would be God's Son, Jesus.

Soon it was almost nighttime. Mary was tired! *How much farther do we have to go?* she might have thought. Finally they saw the town of Bethlehem ahead.

But when Mary and Joseph got to Bethlehem, the town was FULL of people! There was no place for them to sleep. Every room was full. So Mary and Joseph went to a stable where animals were kept. They slept on the hay.

There in the stable, in the quiet nighttime, baby Jesus was born. Mary wrapped baby Jesus in warm clothes. Then she laid Him on soft hay in the manger. (A manger is a box where food is put for animals to eat. It made a comfortable bed for baby Jesus.)

Mary and Joseph took good care of baby Jesus. They were glad Jesus was born. Jesus is God's special Son!

Shepherd Scenes

Collect

Bible, scissors, construction paper, chenille wire, glue, cotton balls.

Prepare

Cut construction paper into geometric shapes (circles, triangles, squares, rectangles, etc.).

Do

Give each child a sheet of construction paper. Children glue geometric shapes together to create a shepherd. Children shape chenille wire to form a staff and glue to picture. Children glue cotton balls to paper to make sheep.

Shepherds at the Stable

Luke 2:8-20

I can tell the good news that Jesus was born.

Enrichment Ideas

1. Children use black construction paper for background. Children stick stars on paper to create a nighttime scene.

2. Instead of geometric shapes, children use markers to draw shepherds on paper.

3. Children draw sheep outlines and then glue cotton balls onto sheep.

Talk About

☼ In today's Bible story, shepherds were taking care of their sheep. Suddenly, angels came and told them that Jesus was born! Jesus is God's Son. The shepherds told others the good news that Jesus was born. Let's make shepherd scenes to remind us of the good news.

☼ Frank, thank you for passing cotton balls to Anisa. You have many sheep in your picture. Shepherds heard the good news that Jesus was born. Who are some people that you can tell about Jesus?

☼ At Christmastime, we can tell others the good news that Jesus was born. Grace, who do you want to tell the good news about Jesus?

shepherds at the Stable

Luke 2:8-20

One quiet night a long time ago, some shepherds were outside taking care of their sheep.

All at once, the sky was full of light. The shepherds looked up and saw an angel! The shepherds were afraid.

But the angel said, "Do not be afraid. I have good news. God's Son, Jesus, has been born. You can go see Him. He is in a stable, wrapped up warm and lying in a manger." (A stable is like a barn. It is the place where animals sleep.) Baby Jesus was lying in a manger. (A manger is a box where food is put for animals to eat.)

Then the sky was FULL of angels! The angels said, "Glory to God!" The angels were thanking God for sending Jesus.

Then the angels left. The shepherds said, "Let's go find this special baby. Let's hurry!" Step-step-step. The shepherds hurried along the road until they found the stable where Jesus was.

The baby Jesus was lying in a manger where the animals usually ate. Everything was just as the angel had said. The shepherds were so happy to see baby Jesus!

Then the shepherds started walking back to take care of their sheep. Along the way, they told the good news to everyone they saw. "Jesus is born! Jesus is born!" The shepherds thanked God for sending Jesus.

Christmas Garland

Collect

Bible, butcher paper, green marker, construction paper in a variety of colors, scissors, glue.

Prepare

Draw a garland on butcher paper. Cut construction paper into circle and/or bell shapes approximately 3 inches (7.5 cm) in size.

Do

Children glue circle and/or bells shapes as ornaments onto the drawn garland. Display decorated garland in classroom.

Jesus Is Welcomed

Luke 2:21-38

I can thank God for Jesus, the Savior.

Talk About

☺ In our Bible story today Simeon and Anna thanked God that Jesus was born. Simeon knew that Jesus was the Savior he had been waiting to see. Anna knew Jesus was the Savior, too. Anna was happy and told people in the Temple about Jesus. Let's make some Christmas decorations to celebrate Jesus' birthday.

☺ Cassidy, what are some other decorations people use at Christmastime? Gina, what are some decorations your family puts up at Christmastime to celebrate Jesus' birthday?

☺ Let's thank God for Jesus. Pray briefly, Thank You, God, for sending Jesus.

Enrichment Ideas

1. Provide seasonal cookie cutters or stencils, pencils, construction paper in a variety of colors and scissors. Children trace around cookie cutters or stencils and cut them out to make ornaments for the garland.

2. Children draw and color decorations onto garland using glitter or gel pens, and markers.

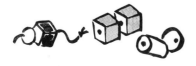

Jesus Is Welcomed

Luke 2:21-38

Simeon was an old man who lived in Jerusalem. He loved God and was often at the Temple, praying and singing praises to God. God had promised Simeon that before he died, he would see God's chosen Son who would save people from their sins.

One day Simeon was at the Temple. He saw Mary and Joseph bringing baby Jesus to be dedicated at the Temple. Parents did this when they wanted their children to love and obey God. Most people probably did not even notice baby Jesus. But Simeon ran up to Mary and Joseph. God helped Simeon know this baby was Jesus, the Savior he had been waiting to see!

Simeon took Jesus in his arms and praised God. He said how wonderful it was to see the promised Savior. Simeon thanked God for Jesus. Mary and Joseph were amazed to hear Simeon's words!

Then a lady named Anna came up. Anna loved God. She saw Simeon holding the baby. She, too, knew this baby was the promised Savior. Anna was very happy. Anna told the people in the Temple that the Savior had come, just as God had promised! Anna thanked God for Jesus.

Toothpick Stars

Wise Men Give Gifts

Matthew 2:1-12

I can give thanks to God for Jesus.

Collect

Bible, construction paper, colored toothpicks, glue.

Prepare

Make a sample star picture.

Do

Children make stars on construction paper by placing colored toothpicks in a dot of glue, points together. (Note: Put away sample picture you made so that as children begin activity, they will be prevented from copying your work.)

Talk About

☼ In today's Bible story, wise men followed a star and found Jesus. They gave Jesus gifts and thanked God for Jesus. Let's make star pictures. Our pictures will remind us to thank God for Jesus.

☼ Amber, what color are the stars you are making? The wise men saw a bright star in the sky. They were glad to see Jesus.

☼ God showed how much He loved us when He sent Jesus to be born. What are some other things God gives us to show how much He loves us? Let's thank God for loving us. Pray briefly.

Enrichment Ideas

1. In addition to or instead of gluing toothpicks, on their papers children trace around star-shaped cookie cutters. Then children color star shapes.

2. Provide gel pens for children to use in drawing stars on black paper.

3. Instead of gluing toothpicks, children place star stickers on a sheet of dark blue, black or dark purple construction paper.

Wise Men Give Gifts

Matthew 2:1-12

Clop, clop, clop went the camels' feet. The camels carried the wise men on their backs. The wise men had seen a very bright star high in the sky. They knew the star meant a special child had been born. The wise men wanted to see this special child.

After many nights, the wise men came to a big city. "Where is the special child God has sent?" the wise men asked everyone they met. "We saw His star. We want to see Him."

"The special child is to be born in Bethlehem," a man told the wise men. "Bethlehem is close by," said the wise men. "Let's hurry and find the child." The wise men climbed up on the camels' backs and started toward Bethlehem.

"Look!" said one wise men as they came to the town. "There's the star!" As the wise men got closer, the star shone above one house. The wise men got down off the camels' backs. They opened their saddlebags and carefully took out beautiful gifts. The wise men found Mary and Jesus. Jesus was a little boy now. The wise men gave Jesus their gifts. They gave Him gold and some sweet-smelling perfumes.

The wise men were glad to see Jesus. They must have been very thankful to God for Jesus.

Gift-Wrap Collages

Collect

Bible, scissors, seasonal wrapping paper, ribbon, construction paper, glue.

Prepare

Cut wrapping paper and ribbon into pieces.

Do

Give each child a sheet of construction paper. Invite children to glue pieces of wrapping paper and ribbon on construction paper to make collages.

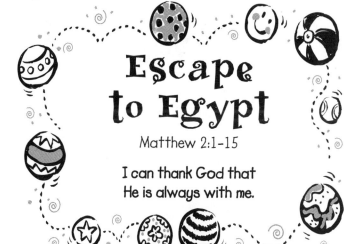

Escape to Egypt

Matthew 2:1-15

I can thank God that He is always with me.

Talk About

☺ Today's Bible story tells about some wise men who packed special gifts and started on a long trip to find God's Son, Jesus. Let's use some gift wrap and ribbon to remind us of the wise men's gifts to Jesus.

☺ DeShawna, this ribbon reminds me of a birthday party. Whose birthday are we celebrating right now? Yes, it is Jesus' birthday. I am glad God sent Jesus and that He is always with us.

☺ These collages remind us of giving gifts. At Christmastime God gave us a gift. He gave us Jesus. Delores, who has given you a gift? What was it? I am glad God loves us and sent His Son, Jesus, to be with us.

Enrichment Ideas

1. Older children cut wrapping paper and ribbon pieces.

2. Before class, cut shapes from seasonal greeting cards. Children add shapes to collages.

3. Give children stamp pads and seasonal stamps. Invite children to add stamp designs to their collage.

Escape to Egypt

Matthew 2:1-15

Jesus had been born in Bethlehem. And God wanted some men far away to know about Jesus' birth. So God put a very bright star in the sky. The star showed the wise men that a great new King had been born!

"Let's go and find this King!" the wise men said. "We'll take special gifts to give the new King." The wise men packed their camels. They rode for days and days.

The wise men went to King Herod's palace. They asked King Herod, "Where is the new King? We saw His star. We want to worship Him."

King Herod got angry! He wanted to be the ONLY king! King Herod asked his helpers where this new King would be born. "God's Word says He will be born in Bethlehem," they said.

King Herod told the wise men, "Go. Find the child. Then come and tell me. I want to worship Him, too." But King Herod really wanted to hurt Jesus!

The wise men went to Bethlehem. They saw the bright star right over Jesus' house! When the wise men saw Jesus, they bowed. They gave Him the special gifts they'd brought. Then God told the wise men in a dream, "Do NOT go back to King Herod." The wise men went home by another road. They never told King Herod where Jesus was!

Soon after the wise men left, an angel talked to Joseph in a dream. "Get up," the angel said. "Take Mary and Jesus to Egypt. King Herod wants to hurt Jesus." Joseph woke Mary and they packed a few things. Mary, Joseph and Jesus started for Egypt in the quiet nighttime. They traveled for many days. Finally, they were in Egypt. Joseph and Mary and Jesus were safe! God was with them.

Sandy Scenes

Collect

Bible, dry sand (or cornmeal or salt), shallow baking dishes, newspaper, glue, cotton swabs, dark-colored construction paper; optional—dry tempera paints.

Prepare

Pour sand into baking dishes. (Note: Prepare one setup for every three or four children.) (Optional: Mix sand and tempera together, each color in a separate baking dish.) Cover tables with newspaper.

Do

Children spread glue with cotton swabs to make designs on sheets of construction paper. Then children sprinkle sand over papers to cover glue. (Optional: Children sprinkle colored sand over glued paper.) When glue has been completely covered, assist children in carefully lifting papers and pouring sand back into baking dishes. Sand will adhere to glued areas.

Enrichment Ideas

1. Use glue to print the word "Jesus" on children's papers. Children sprinkle sand over glue.

2. Instead of making pictures on papers, children use fingers to draw designs in damp sand. Prepare a pie tin or flat-bottomed bowl with about a half inch of sand in the bottom for each child.

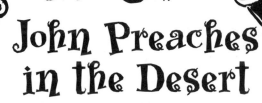

John Preaches in the Desert

Matthew 3:1-6; Mark 1:1-8; Luke 3:1-18

I can learn to obey God and do good things.

Talk About

☼ In today's Bible story, a man lived in the desert and told people to obey God and do good things. Deserts have a lot of sand. Let's make pictures with sand.

☼ Maribel, thank you for waiting for your turn to use the sand. You know how to do good things! What are some other good things you can do in our classroom?

☼ Andrew, thank you for doing a good thing by sharing your glue. We can learn to obey God and do good things. What is a good thing you can do at your home?

John Preaches in the Desert

Matthew 3:1-6; Mark 1:1-8; Luke 3:1-18

Jesus had a cousin named John. John lived in the desert all by himself. John wore clothes made of scratchy camel hair and he wore a leather belt. He ate food he found in the desert: insects like grasshoppers, and sweet honey.

God had a special job for John. God wanted John to tell people that Jesus is God's Son.

John stayed near the Jordan River. He told people to get ready for Jesus. John told people, "God will forgive you for doing wrong things. But stop doing wrong things. Do good things."

People wanted to know good things to do. They asked John, "What should we do?"

John answered, "If you have two coats, give one coat to a person who has no coat. If you have extra food, give some to hungry people."

John told some other people more ways to do what is right. "Don't take money that doesn't belong to you," he said. He told some soldiers, "Don't say someone did wrong when you know that person did NOT do anything wrong. Tell only what is true."

Many people listened to John. They stopped doing wrong things. They promised to do what is right. Then John baptized them. He used water to show that God forgives people for the wrong things they do. John helped many, many people learn to obey God and do good things.

River Pictures

Collect

Bible, white construction paper, markers, blue cellophane, tape.

Do

Children draw river items on papers (stones, fish, small plants, etc.). Give each child a sheet of blue cellophane a little smaller than paper. Help children tape cellophane over papers to make river pictures.

John Baptizes Jesus

Matthew 3:13-17; Mark 1:9-11;
Luke 3:21-22; John 1:19-34

I'm glad God sent His Son, Jesus.

Talk About

☼ In our Bible story today, a man named John told people that Jesus is God's Son. John was glad to know that Jesus is God's Son. John and Jesus and many people were standing by a river. Jesus wanted to obey God by being baptized in the river. Let's make river pictures to remind us about today's story.

☼ Merissa, I see you used the blue marker to draw a river. When have you been to a river? What did you see in the river?

☼ I am glad to know that God sent His Son, Jesus. Jesus loves everyone in the world. Thank You, God, for Your Son, Jesus.

Enrichment Ideas

1. Provide paper and scissors. Children draw river items on paper, cut them out and glue them to their pictures.

2. Provide glue, small pebbles and bits of plants for children to glue to their river pictures before covering them with cellophane.

John Baptizes Jesus

Matthew 3:13-17; Mark 1:9-11; Luke 3:21-22; John 1:19-34

John was telling people about God. John said that God would soon send His Son. "Get ready for the One God promised to send," John said.

Many, many people came to hear John. John told the people they needed to tell God they were sorry for doing wrong. John baptized many people with water to show that they were sorry for doing wrong.

Some leaders heard about John. They sent messengers to talk to John. They asked, "Are you the One God promised to send?"

John said, "No. I am not the One God promised to send. I was sent to get the people ready for Him. God is about to send Him. The One God will send is much more important than I am!"

One day, Jesus came to John. He asked John to baptize Him. John said, "I need You to baptize me! You don't need to be baptized."

Jesus said, "This is what God wants us to do. I want to obey God."

So John baptized Jesus. Then something surprising happened! From heaven, God's Spirit, looking like a dove, came down to Jesus.

God spoke from heaven. "This is My Son, whom I love. I am pleased with Him!" This had never happened before. Everyone was amazed.

The next day, John saw Jesus. John pointed to Jesus. "There He is," John said. "Look. Jesus will forgive people for the wrong things they have done!" Jesus was the One God had promised to send. Jesus is God's Son.

Boats in the Water

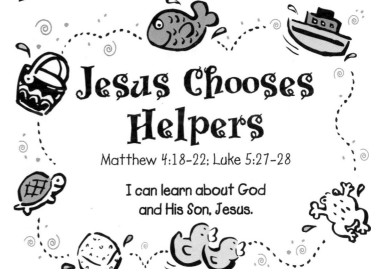

Jesus Chooses Helpers

Matthew 4:18-22; Luke 5:27-28

I can learn about God and His Son, Jesus.

Collect

Bible; brown, white and blue construction paper; markers; scissors; tape; paper fasteners.

Prepare

For each child, draw a boat on brown paper and a sail outline on white paper.

Do

Child cuts out boat and sail and tapes them together. Help each child accordion-fold a sheet of blue paper to make water. Use a paper fastener to attach boat to water. Children rock boats back and forth.

Talk About

☺ In our Bible story, Jesus asked four men who were fishermen to be His helpers. The four men used boats when they went fishing. Today we are going to make boats to help us remember the story of Jesus' helpers.

☺ Sophia, who helps you learn about God and His Son, Jesus? We can learn about Jesus when we hear and obey God's Word, the Bible.

☺ When Jesus asked the fishermen to follow Him, they obeyed! They wanted to learn about God and His Son, Jesus. What did you learn about Jesus today, Esteban?

Enrichment Ideas

1. Children place fish stickers on waves or draw and cut out paper fish to glue to waves.

2. Children draw waves on white paper. Instead of making a stand-up scene, children attach boats to white paper with paper fasteners.

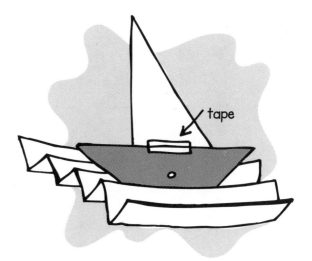

tape

Jesus Chooses Helpers

Matthew 4:18-22; Luke 5:27-28

One day Jesus walked by the big blue Sea of Galilee. He saw some fishermen in their boats. They were throwing their big fishing nets out into the water. Jesus knew two of these fishermen.

"Peter! Andrew!" Jesus called. Peter and Andrew looked to see who was calling their names. When they saw Jesus, they pulled their nets into their boat. They hurried to see Jesus.

When Peter and Andrew came to the beach, Jesus said, "Come and help Me tell people about God." Peter and Andrew obeyed. They went with Jesus. They wanted to learn more about Him. They wanted to help others learn about Jesus, too. Now Jesus had two helpers.

Later Jesus and His two friends saw two other fishermen. "James and John!" Jesus called. "Come with Me!" Right away, James and John went, too. They were glad to go with Jesus. Now Jesus had four helpers.

On another day, Jesus walked by a man named Matthew. Matthew was at work. "Follow Me, Matthew," said Jesus. Matthew got right up. He left everything! Now Jesus had FIVE friends to help Him! On other days, Jesus asked other people to be His helpers—until He had 1, 2, 3, 4, 5, 6, 7, 8, 9, 10, 11, 12 helpers.

Jesus told His 12 helpers many things about God. Jesus' friends did just what Jesus said to do. They helped people learn about God and His Son, Jesus.

Prayer Reminders

Collect

Bible, 4x10-inch (10x25.5-cm) construction paper rectangles, pencil, markers, tape.

Prepare

Fold one rectangle for each child (see sketch a). Make a sample prayer reminder.

Do

On rectangles, trace around each child's hands (left hand on one side, right hand on the other) with hands flat. Children decorate their hands. Fold and tape rectangles to make stand-up prayer reminders for children to take home (see sketch b).

Enrichment Ideas

1. Each child writes his or her name on one side of the prayer reminder. Print the phrase "prays to God" on the other side.

2. Provide glitter pens, paint, stickers, etc. for children to decorate their hands.

3. Brush a thin layer of paint on child's hands. Children make print with each hand on rectangles.

Jesus' Prayer

Matthew 6:5-13;

Mark 1:35-37; Luke 11:1-4

I can talk to God and tell Him I love Him.

Talk About

☺ In today's Bible story, Jesus taught people to pray to God. When we pray, we can thank God for the good things He has done for us. Let's make some prayer reminders to help us remember to pray.

☺ I see you are using the markers to color your hands. I'm thankful that God loves us and gives us hands. Linda, what are some things you are thankful for? Let's tell God that we love Him and thank Him for the good things He gives us. *Pray briefly.*

☺ I'm glad to thank God. Saying "Thank You" to God shows that I love Him. Pearl, when are some times you and your family talk to God?

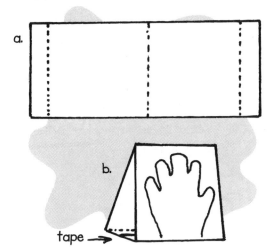

a.

b.

tape →

Jesus' Prayer

Matthew 6:5-13; Mark 1:35-37; Luke 11:1-4

One day, Jesus had made many sick people well. And all day long, Jesus had been telling people about God's love. Now it was bed-time. Jesus went to bed in a house with His friends.

When it was morning, many people came to see Jesus. Jesus' friends went to find Jesus. They probably called His name, but Jesus didn't answer. *Where is Jesus?* His friends must have wondered. Jesus' friends looked inside and outside the house. They STILL did not find Jesus.

So Jesus' friends walked down the road to find Jesus. Soon they came to a quiet place. They saw Jesus there, all alone. He was praying. He was talking to God. Jesus often prayed by Himself.

One day, one of Jesus' friends asked, "Will You teach us to pray?"

"Yes," Jesus said, "I will teach you to pray."

Jesus said, "When you pray, pray like this:

'Our Father in heaven, You are so good. I pray that all people will obey You. Give us what we need each day. Forgive the wrong things we do. We forgive people who do wrong to us. Help us to do right. You are the King. You can do anything. Amen.'"

Jesus told His friends that we can talk to God in the same way we talk to a kind, loving father. Jesus told us to ask our Father for what we need. Jesus said we should ask God to forgive the wrong things we do. And we should forgive other people for wrong things they do to us. We can ask God to help us do right things. We can tell God how much we love Him.

Flower Gardens

Collect

Bible, a length of butcher paper, markers, glue, muffin cup liners.

Do

Place paper on floor or tabletop. Invite children to create a garden scene by drawing flowers or gluing muffin cup liners to drawn stems to create flowers on the paper.

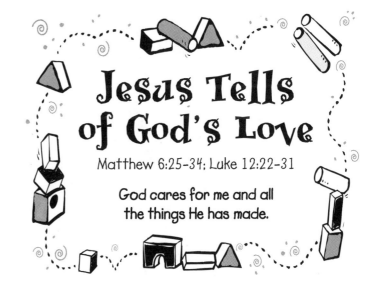

Jesus Tells of God's Love

Matthew 6:25-34; Luke 12:22-31

God cares for me and all the things He has made.

Enrichment Ideas

1. Each child chooses a number between four and eight and then draws flowers having the chosen number of petals.

2. Before class, cut flower petals from green construction paper. Children glue green chenille wire under flowers for stems and glue petals along the length of stems.

Talk About

☺ Today in our Bible story, Jesus told about the ways God cares for flowers. We are going to make a flower garden to help us remember how God cares for flowers and that He cares for us even more.

☺ Max, I see you are drawing blue flowers. What does God send to help flowers grow? (Rain. Sun.) God takes care of flowers. God takes care of you, too. Who does God give you to help you?

☺ Kelli, who lives with you? God cares for you by giving you a mom and a dad. Let's thank Him. Pray briefly.

Jesus Tells of God's Love

Matthew 6:25-34; Luke 12:22-31

One day Jesus was sitting on a hill talking with His friends. "Look at those birds up in the sky," Jesus said. "Just think about those birds." Jesus' friends watched as the birds flew high in the air. The birds ate the grain that grew in the fields. At night they had a place to sleep in the trees.

"Those birds don't plant the seeds they eat," Jesus said. "But God, your Father in heaven, feeds each one. He cares about them."

Then Jesus might have bent down and picked a beautiful flower. "Think about the way the flowers grow," Jesus said. "Flowers don't sew their leaves onto their stems with a needle and thread. Yet even kings do not wear clothes as beautiful as this flower." Jesus' friends listened.

Then Jesus said, "God makes beautiful flowers. And He cares about them. He sends rain. He sends the warm sun to help the flowers grow. If God does that for the flowers, He will surely take care of you! He loves you much more than birds and flowers. Do not worry about what to eat or what to wear. Our Father in heaven knows just what you need. Always try to love and obey God. He will take care of you. He loves you."

Stormy Weather

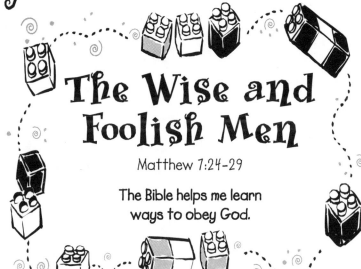

The Wise and Foolish Men

Matthew 7:24-29

The Bible helps me learn ways to obey God.

Collect

Bible, butcher paper, measuring stick, scissors, black and blue markers; optional—yarn, masking tape.

Prepare

For each group of two or three children, cut a 2- to 4-foot (.6- to 1.2-m) long cloud shape from butcher paper.

Do

Children use markers to decorate cloud shapes and make storm clouds. (Optional: Use yarn and masking tape to suspend storm clouds from classroom ceiling or mount on walls.)

Enrichment Ideas

1. Cut large raindrops from gray paper. Children glue raindrops to strands of tinsel or yarn. Tape strands to hang from clouds.

2. Provide blue and white cotton balls. Children glue cotton balls to cloud shapes.

3. Before class, color water with blue food coloring. Put eyedroppers and blue water in small cups. Children use eyedroppers to squeeze raindrops onto white construction paper. Children draw clouds around raindrops.

Talk About

☺ Our Bible story today told about two men. One man was wise and built a house on rock. The other man was foolish and built a house on the sand. In a big rainstorm, the house on the sand fell down. This story reminds us to be wise and obey God's words. Let's make storm clouds to help us remember this story.

☺ I like the way you shared markers, Tish. Sharing is a way to obey God's words. What are some other things you can share?

☺ God gave us His words in the Bible to help us learn ways to obey Him. Lizzie, helping is a way to obey God's words. What are ways you can help?

The Wise and Foolish Men

Matthew 7:24-29

One day Jesus told a story about building a house. He said, "A wise man built his house on a strong rock. Then the rain came, the river rose, and the winds blew! But the house did not fall down. It was built on strong rock. This wise man is like a person who listens to Me and obeys My words."

"But," said Jesus, "a foolish man built his house on the sand. When the rain and winds came, the house on the sand fell down. It wasn't built on something strong. A person who hears My words but won't follow them is like this foolish man."

Jesus told this story about the wise and foolish men to help people learn how important it is to obey God's words. God's words are true and help people know the best way to live. We can read God's words in the Bible.

Scratch-and-Sniff Paintings

Collect

Bible, unsweetened drink mix packages, scissors, shallow bowls, water, tablespoon, plastic spoons, paintbrushes, paper.

Do

Children help each other make scratch-and-sniff paint by taking turns to complete the following tasks: Cut open and pour drink mixes into individual bowls. Add one tablespoon of water to each mix. Stir water and mix. Children paint pictures and allow to dry. When paint is dry, children may scratch and sniff the paint.

Enrichment Ideas

1. Children paint pictures of places where they may help others (home, school, playground, church, etc.).

2. Children help to use leftover drink mix to make a drink in a large pitcher. Pour drink into small pitchers so that children can pour into small paper cups.

Woman at the Well

John 4:3-42

Jesus knows all about me and loves me.

Talk About

☺ In today's Bible story, a woman went to a well to get water. A well is a deep hole in the ground. People dip buckets into a well to get water. Let's use water to make some good-smelling paint.

☺ We don't need to dip buckets in a hole to get water at our homes. Anne, what are some ways you get water at your house? Jesus knows about us and loves us. He gives us good things to drink.

☺ Scott, what are some of the ways you use water at your house? Giving water to your brother to drink is a good thing to do. Jesus knows and loves you and your brother. Jesus cares for you.

Woman at the Well

John 4:3-42

Step-step-step. Jesus and His friends walked and walked along the hot, dusty road. Soon they came to a well of cool water. (A well is a deep hole in the ground. People dip buckets in a well to get water.) Jesus stopped by the well to rest. His friends walked into a nearby town to buy food.

While Jesus was resting, a woman came to the well. She was carrying a big jar. The woman came to get water from the well. "Will you please give me a drink of water?" Jesus asked her.

The woman was surprised when Jesus talked to her. She did not know who Jesus was. Then Jesus began to talk about God. The woman listened carefully. Jesus knew all about this woman. Jesus told her about things she had done.

The woman wondered how this man knew all about her. She said, "I know that God will send someone to help us understand what is true.

Jesus said, "I am the One that God promised to send."

The woman was so happy to hear this good news! She left her water jar by the well. She hurried into town. "Come!" she told the people. "Come see a man who knows all about me! Do you think He was sent by God?"

Many people came with the woman. They wanted to see Jesus. They wanted to hear what He said. "Stay and tell us more," the people said to Jesus. Jesus stayed in their town two days. Jesus told them about God's love. Many people believed what Jesus said, and they loved Jesus, too.

Heart Art

Collect

Bible, paper plates, hole punch, markers, yarn or ribbon, scissors, measuring stick, transparent tape.

Prepare

For each child, punch holes around edge of a paper plate. Draw heart shape in center of each plate. For each child, cut a 3-foot (.9-m) length of yarn. Tie one end of yarn to a hole in a paper plate. Wrap other end of yarn with transparent tape to make a needle.

Do

1. Children sew around paper plate by threading yarn through holes. As they finish, assist children in tying a knot to secure their stitches.

2. Children decorate plates with markers.

Enrichment Ideas

1. Before class, do not draw hearts on the paper plates, but prepare several heart patterns: Use a heart-shaped cookie cutter to trace hearts on poster board; cut out hearts. Older children use patterns to trace hearts on their paper plates.

2. Instead of sewing around plate edges, children use heart-shaped stickers and/or rubber stamps and washable-ink pad to decorate heart plates.

A Sick Boy Is Made Well

John 4:46-53

Jesus teaches me about God's love.

Talk About

☺ In today's Bible story, a man went to see Jesus because his son was sick. Jesus made the son well again. Jesus loved the man and his son. Jesus loves us, too. Let's make some hearts to remind us of how much Jesus loves us.

☺ Nancy, I see you colored your heart purple. These hearts remind us of God's love for us. Who are some people God loves?

☺ Reading Bible stories is a good way to learn what Jesus teaches us. Tony, who reads Bible stories to you? Your grandpa is helping you learn about Jesus.

A Sick Boy Is Made Well

John 4:46-53

Our Bible tells about a boy who was very sick. He was hot with fever. His father must have done all he could to take good care of his sick boy. But the little boy did not get better. He was still very, very sick.

How sad I am! thought the little boy's father. *My son is so sick.* The father wanted to help his sick son. Then he remembered that a man named Jesus made sick people well. *I must find Jesus. He can make my son well,* the father thought. And off he went to find Jesus.

The father walked and he walked and he walked some more. Finally he reached the town where Jesus was. Many people were listening to Jesus. The father ran up to Jesus. "I have been looking for You, Jesus. You must come to my town!" he cried. "My son is very sick. Please come, or he will die."

Jesus loved the man and He loved the man's son. "You may go home," Jesus said. "Your son will live." The man believed Jesus' words. He knew that Jesus' words were true.

The father began to walk home. He was glad his son would be well. While he was walking, he saw some people coming toward him. As the people got closer, the father could see they were his helpers from home. "Sir, your son is well!" they told him. "He will live!"

"I know," the father said. "Jesus made him well."

The man and his helpers were very happy. They were thankful for Jesus' love.

Bible-Times Houses

Collect

Bible, small paper bags, scissors, paper, ruler, markers, transparent tape.

Prepare

For each child, cut a paper bag in half (see sketch a). For each child, cut a 3x10-inch (7.5x25.5-cm) strip of paper. Accordion-fold each strip into steps (see sketch b).

Do

With paper bags folded flat and the bottom of the bag at the top, children use markers to draw windows and a door. Children open paper bags and turn upside down to form Bible-times houses. (Optional: Children cut doors open.) Assist children to tape paper stairs to the sides of their houses (see sketch c).

Enrichment Ideas

1. Cut a three-sided opening in the roof of each paper-bag house. Older children use toy people to act out the story action as you briefly retell story events. Expect to repeat the story several times as children complete their houses.

2. Instead of making individual houses, provide a cardboard box. Fold paper and tape to side of box to make stairs as described above. Children use markers to decorate box. (Note: Provide one box for every group of three or four children.)

Friends Help a Lame Man

Mark 2:1-12

Jesus teaches me to be kind.

Talk About

☺ Our Bible tells us about four men who had a friend who couldn't walk. The four men took their friend to see Jesus. Jesus was kind and made the man well. Jesus was staying in a house that had a flat roof. Let's make houses with flat roofs, too!

☺ Brynne, I see you handed Marta a marker. You know how to help others! Helping others is a good way to be kind.

☺ Jesus teaches us to be kind to others. He will help us to be kind, even when it is hard. What are some ways for you to be kind, Oscar?

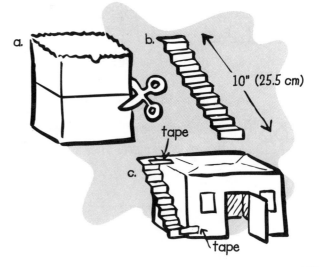

a.

b.

10" (25.5 cm)

tape

c.

tape

Friends Help a Lame Man

Mark 2:1-12

Our Bible tells about a man who was lame. That means he couldn't walk. He couldn't even stand up! He could only lie on his mat and wait for his kind friends to help him. The sick man wanted to be well—to sit up, to stand and to walk all by himself!

One day this man's four friends heard that Jesus was in their town. "If only he could go to see Jesus," the friends must have said to each other. "Surely Jesus could make our friend well!"

So the four friends picked up the man on his mat. They carried him as they walked down the road to see Jesus. But when they got to the house where Jesus was talking, it was packed full of people. Many people wanted to see Jesus. There wasn't any room inside! People were even standing in the doorway. Other people stood outside, looking in the windows.

The four friends must have felt sad. There was just no way to get in—not even for one person and especially not for the four of them and their friend lying on his mat.

Then the friends remembered the flat roof on top of the house. The friends climbed the stairs outside the house to the roof. They carried their friend with them. The four friends began to pull away pieces of the roof. Finally the hole was big enough! Carefully the friends lowered the man down, down into the house. Soon he was right in front of Jesus.

Jesus loved the man. "Stand up, take your mat, and walk," Jesus told him. And the man did just that! How happy he was that Jesus had made him well! How thankful he was for his kind friends! All the people in the house were surprised! All the people thanked God.

Big Storms

Collect

Bible, ½-inch (1.3-cm) wide foil strips, cotton balls, construction paper in dark colors, glue.

Do

Children make storm scenes by bending foil into lightning zigzags and stretching out cotton balls to make clouds. Children glue lightning and clouds to paper.

Jesus Stops the Storm

Matthew 8:23-27; Mark 4:1,35-41

I can ask Jesus for help because of His great power.

Enrichment Ideas

1. Children dictate sentences about their storm scenes. Print sentences on separate paper. Staple paper to back of each child's storm scene.

2. Children glue glitter or color with glitter pens to make sparkly raindrops on their papers.

3. Children roll small pieces of blue tissue into little balls and glue to paper for raindrops.

Talk About

☀ In our Bible story today, Jesus and His friends were in a big storm. Jesus' friends were VERY afraid! But Jesus told the storm to stop, and it did! Jesus helped His friends when they were afraid. Let's make some stormy pictures to remind us of Jesus' great power and help.

☀ Dusty, are you making clouds or lightning? Sometimes it's fun to be out in the rain, but sometimes it can be scary! Why might a storm be scary? When we are afraid, we can ask Jesus to help us.

☀ Jesus is strong and powerful. Jesus can help us when we feel afraid. When are some times you feel afraid and can ask Jesus for help?

Jesus Stops the Storm

Matthew 8:23-27; Mark 4:1,35-41

One night Jesus and His friends were sailing across the lake in their boat. Jesus was very tired. He lay down in the back of the boat. Soon He was asleep.

Suddenly, the wind began to blow. Ooooo! Ooooo! The wind blew harder and harder. The little waves got bigger and bigger. Splish! Splish-splash! Splash! The big waves hit hard against the little boat. Water splashed into the boat. Splash! Splash! Splash! The boat was filling with water.

"I'm afraid!" one of Jesus' friends shouted.

"Jesus! Help us!" shouted another friend. "Don't You care that our boat is sinking?!"

Jesus woke up. He felt the strong winds blowing. He saw the big waves splashing. Jesus stood up and said, "Quiet! Be still!" And just like that, the wind stopped blowing. The big waves stopped splashing. Splish. Splish. Little waves rocked the boat gently again.

"Why were you so afraid?" Jesus asked His friends. "Don't you know that I love you?"

Jesus' friends looked at each other. They said, "Wow! Even the winds and the waves obey Jesus!" They were glad Jesus could take care of them and help them when they were afraid.

Edible Jewelry

Jesus Feeds 5,000

Mark 6:30-44; John 6:1-14

I'm thankful to Jesus for His love and the good things He gives me.

Collect

Bible, yarn, scissors, measuring stick, circle-shaped dry cereal, transparent tape, paper, marker.

Prepare

Cut one 2- to 3-foot (.6- to .9-m) length of yarn for each child. Tie a piece of cereal to one end. Wrap the other end with tape for children to use as a needle.

Post a note alerting parents to the use of food in this activity. Also check registration forms for possible food allergies.

Do

Children string cereal onto yarn. When each child is finished, tie necklace loosely around child's neck so that necklace can be lifted on and off over the child's head.

Enrichment Ideas

1. In addition to necklaces, older children make wristbands. Help children tie wristbands around wrists.

2. Provide pretzel rings and hollow licorice pieces. Invite children to string pretzels and licorice to make necklaces.

Talk About

☼ In today's Bible story, Jesus showed love for a crowd of people. He helped them have food to eat. Let's make necklaces we can eat!

☼ When do you usually eat cereal? Tim, what are some other foods you eat at breakfast? I'm glad Jesus gives us lots of good things to eat!

☼ God gives us more than good food. He also gives us people to love and care for us. Who are some of the people God has given you? What is something they do to take care of you?

Jesus Feeds 5,000

Mark 6:30-44; John 6:1-14

Jesus sat down to rest on a hillside one day. A big crowd of people—lots and lots and lots of people—came to see Him. The people wanted to hear Jesus talk about God. They listened to Jesus until suppertime. Jesus knew these people were hungry. "Where can we buy food for all these people?" Jesus said to His friends.

"We don't have enough money to buy food for all these people!" one of Jesus' friends said.

Just then another friend said, "Here is a boy who has five little loaves of bread and two fish."

"But that's not enough food for all these people," another friend might have said.

Jesus picked up the little boy's lunch. He thanked God. He began to break the bread and fish into pieces. And the most surprising thing happened! Soon there were hundreds and hundreds of pieces of bread and fish! There was enough bread and fish to give to all those hungry people. Every person had plenty to eat.

When everybody had finished eating, Jesus' friends gathered up 12 baskets of leftover bread and fish. Jesus had made enough food out of that little boy's lunch to feed all those people—and still have lots of food left over! What a wonderful way for Jesus to show His love to people! The people were very glad and very thankful.

Jesus Puppets

Collect

Bible, paper lunch bags, markers.

Do

Each child makes a paper-bag Jesus puppet by drawing a mouth on the edge of the fold and drawing other facial details on top portion of bag. Children draw clothing on bottom portion of bag. Child moves bag and says Jesus' words "Serve others."

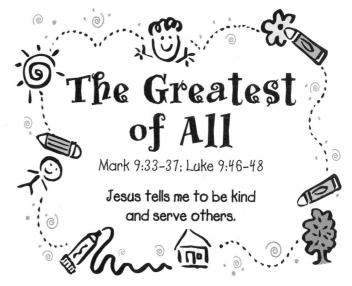

The Greatest of All

Mark 9:33-37; Luke 9:46-48

Jesus tells me to be kind and serve others.

Enrichment Ideas

1. Children make puppets for other characters in the story (Jesus' friends and the boy). Read the Bible story from Mark 9:33-37. Children move puppets to illustrate story action.

2. Provide children with scissors, glue, construction paper, fabric and yarn. Children make beards, clothes and hair to glue onto Jesus puppet.

Talk About

☼ In our Bible story today, Jesus told His friends that to be a great person, they should serve others. Serving others means we are kind and help others. Let's make Jesus puppets to help us remember what Jesus tells us about serving others.

☼ How can we be kind and serve each other in our class? Nathaniel, that's right! We can serve each other by sharing markers.

☼ When you were getting ready to come to church today, who helped you? How? Alana, your mother was kind and served you by fixing your breakfast.

The Greatest of All

Mark 9:33-37; Luke 9:46-48

Jesus and His friends traveled from place to place. As they walked, Jesus' friends talked. One day, instead of using words that were happy and friendly, Jesus' friends said words that were unkind! One of Jesus' friends must have said he was better than someone else. Pretty soon each of them was feeling ANGRY! Each one wanted to be the greatest, or the best!

Jesus and His friends came into a house. Jesus said to His friends, "What were you arguing about on the road?"

Jesus' friends got very quiet. But Jesus KNEW they had been arguing about who was the greatest. And Jesus knew they had some wrong ideas.

Jesus sat down. Then He picked up a little child. Jesus set the child down beside the men. Jesus looked at His friends and said, "If you want God to think you are great, you must be like this little child. Don't think you are better than everyone else."

Jesus' friends were surprised. They thought they had to show God how good they were. Jesus was telling His friends they needed to learn that God loves a little child just as much as He loves any grown-up.

Jesus hugged the little child. He looked around at His friends. He said, "Treat children the way you would treat ME. When you are kind to children, it is the same as being kind to Me. God thinks you are great when you are kind and serve others."

Jesus wanted His friends to treat others with love and kindness instead of worrying about trying to be better than everyone else!

Coin Rubbings

Collect

Bible, crayons, white paper, a variety of coins.

Prepare

Remove the paper from the crayons. Fold each sheet of paper in half widthwise.

Do

Each child places a coin between a folded sheet of white paper, pushing the coin all the way to the fold. Child uses side of crayon to color over the coin, creating a rubbing. Children repeat with other coins. Give children additional paper as needed.

The Forgiving King

Matthew 18:21-35

I show God's love and kindness when I forgive others.

Talk About

☼ Our Bible story today is about a king who let a man borrow lots of money. When the man couldn't pay the money back to the king, the king said he didn't have to give back the money. The king forgave the man. We're making coin rubbings to show lots of money.

☼ Alex, you said, "I'm sorry," when you knocked Justin's crayon on the floor. Justin can be kind and forgive you. You both are showing God's love.

☼ When the king forgave the man, he was kind. The king showed God's love. We can show God's love and be kind, too. Yolanda, who are some people you can be kind to?

Enrichment Ideas

1. Children count how many coin rubbings they made.

2. Instead of placing coins inside folded paper, coins may also be placed inside white letter-sized envelopes to make rubbings.

The Forgiving King

Matthew 18:21-35

Once there was a man who worked for a king. This man had asked the king for lots and lots of money and had promised that he would pay it all back. One day, the king told this man, "Pay back all the money you borrowed from me. And pay me right now!" But the man didn't have the money.

The king was angry. He called one of his helpers. The king told his helper, "Since this man cannot pay me, take everything he has, sell it, and give that money to me!"

The man fell to his knees. "No! No!" the man cried. "I promise to pay you back!" The king felt sorry for this man. "I forgive you," said the king. "You do not have to pay back ANY of the money."

The man must have felt very happy that the king had been so kind. On the way home, the man saw a friend. The friend had borrowed just a LITTLE money from him. The man grabbed his friend and shouted, "Pay back the money you owe me! Pay it back right now." The friend got down on his knees. His friend begged, "Please wait for a little while. I promise to pay you back." But the man would NOT forgive his friend. The man had his friend put in jail.

The king heard that the man had been unkind to his friend. The king told the man to come to see him. The king said to the man, "You are a mean person. I forgave you for ALL the money you owed me. But you would not forgive your friend for just a small amount of money." The king was very angry. He put the unkind man in jail.

After the story, Jesus said, "God is like the king. God forgave you a lot. So God wants you to ALWAYS forgive other people." We can show God's love and kindness when we forgive others.

Color Petals

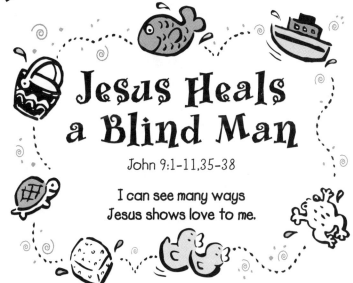

Jesus Heals a Blind Man

John 9:1-11,35-38

I can see many ways
Jesus shows love to me.

Collect

Bible, construction paper in a variety of colors, scissors, ruler, paper plates, glue, markers.

Prepare

Cut construction paper into 1- to 2-inch (2.5- to 5-cm) triangles.

Do

Children choose triangles and glue them to the edges of a paper plate to form a flower. Children use markers to decorate their flowers.

Talk About

☼ In our Bible story today, Jesus showed His love by making a blind man's eyes see. Let's use our eyes while we make colorful flowers.

☼ Zach, what colors are you using to make your flower? God made our eyes so that we can see colors. What else can you do with your eyes? Can you wink? Can you blink? Show me how.

☼ God is good to give us eyes to see! We can see many ways Jesus shows He loves us. Let's name some ways that Jesus shows us that He loves us.

Enrichment Ideas

1. Children glue cotton balls to the centers of their flowers. Spray balls very lightly with a bit of perfume or cologne.

2. To create a flower mural, cut a long sheet of butcher paper. Children glue their flowers to butcher paper and use crayons or markers to draw stems.

Jesus Heals a Blind Man

John 9:1-11,35-38

One day a man was sitting beside the road. He could not see the green grass. He could not see the yellow flowers. He could not see the blue sky. He could not see the children playing. He could not see with his eyes. The man was blind. But he could hear. And this is what he heard: Step-step-step. Step-step-step. The blind man heard someone walking along the road.

The blind man felt someone put cool mud on his eyes. He heard someone say, "Go now and wash in the pool of water." It was Jesus talking to him!

The blind man went right away to the pool and washed the mud off his eyes. As he washed, something wonderful happened!

"I can see!" the man probably shouted. "I can see green grass and yellow flowers. I can see the blue sky. I can see children playing."

Soon people came to see what had happened. "Isn't this the man who was blind?" they asked.

The man was so excited, he must have shouted, "I AM the man who used to be blind! A man named Jesus put mud on my eyes and told me to wash in the pool. I did what He said and now I can see!" And everywhere the man went, he told that Jesus had made his blind eyes see. Jesus showed how much He loved the man.

Shepherd Mural

Collect

Bible, large length of butcher paper, markers, cotton balls; optional—toy person.

Prepare

Draw a sheepfold, a path and some hills on the paper (see sketch).

Do

Place paper on tabletop or floor. Children draw grass, water and trees on paper. Guide children to use cotton balls for sheep and move "sheep" to act out the Bible story. (Optional: Children use toy person as shepherd to help act out story.)

The Good Shepherd

Luke 15:3-7

God loves me and I can show His love and kindness to others.

Enrichment Ideas

1. Print words to label each part of the mural.

2. Children use watercolor paints to paint the mural. When scene is dry, children glue cotton balls to mural for sheep.

3. Before class, cut one sheep shape for each child. In class, children glue cotton balls to precut sheep shapes. Children glue sheep to mural.

Talk About

☺ In our Bible story today, a shepherd took care of 100 sheep. Let's draw some grass and water and trees to show that the shepherd helped his sheep have food and water and shade.

☺ Anna, thank you for giving cotton balls to David. Sharing is a way to show God's love and kindness. Who has shared with you in our classroom?

☺ Because God loves us, we can show love to others. Kelley, who can you show love to?

The Good Shepherd

Luke 15:3-7

One day Jesus told this story. There was a shepherd who had one hundred sheep. (One hundred is *many more than the number of children* in our class!) This shepherd loved his sheep. He knew the name of each one of his sheep.

In the morning the kind shepherd led his sheep to the hillsides. The sheep ate the green grass on the hillside. And they drank cool water. The shepherd made sure the sheep had enough to eat and drink.

When nighttime came, the shepherd kept his sheep safe in a place called a sheepfold. This sheepfold was a big yard with a stone wall around it. There was no door, so the shepherd slept right across the doorway of the sheepfold. "No one can get into the sheepfold and hurt MY sheep!" he said.

One day the shepherd was counting his sheep. He counted 1 . . . 2 . . . 3 . . . all the way up to 98 . . . 99 but oh my! One sheep was GONE! Where was that sheep?

Right away the shepherd went out to find his lost sheep. He looked and looked. He called and called the sheep's name. Then the shepherd heard something. BAAA! *What was that?* he wondered. Then he heard it again. BAAA! That was the lost sheep! The sheep had gotten lost and could not find its way home. The shepherd reached down and lifted the sheep onto his shoulders. All the way home, the kind shepherd carried the sheep. The shepherd was so happy to have found the lost sheep.

"God loves us like that," Jesus said. "He is glad when we choose to love and obey Him."

Beaded Rings

Collect

Bible, chenille wires, scissors, pony beads.

Prepare

Cut each chenille wire into four pieces, one piece for each child.

Do

Children string beads on chenille wires. Help children wrap chenille wires around fingers to make rings. Briefly tell today's Bible story.

The Loving Father

Luke 15:11-24

I show God's love when I am kind to my family and forgive them.

Talk About

☼ Our Bible story today tells about a father who loved his sons. One son went away from home and did wrong things. Later the son was sorry he had done wrong things. He went back home. The father was glad and forgave his son. He gave his son a ring. We're making rings to remind us of this story.

☼ Sean, your ring has four beads on it. It was kind of the father in our story to give his son a ring. Who in your family has been kind to you? What did your dad do?

☼ Rebekah, who is in your family? You are being kind to your little brother when you share a toy with him.

Enrichment Ideas

1. Children make rings for themselves and several extras to give to family members.

2. Instead of making rings, children string circle-shaped cereal on full-length chenille wires to make necklaces or bracelets.

The Loving Father

Luke 15:11-24

Once there was a father with two sons. They lived on a big farm. The father loved his sons. He took good care of them. One day one son said, "Father, you promised to give me money someday. I want it NOW!" So the father gave his son the money.

The son wanted to live far away from his family. The son packed his clothes and began walking away. The father felt sad. While the son was gone, the father waited and waited for the son to come home.

When the son got to a new place, he spent his money until it was all gone. His nice clothes became dirty and torn. Soon he didn't have enough food to eat.

The son went to work feeding some pigs. As he worked, the son thought, *Even the men who work for my father have food to eat.* The son decided, *I'll go back home!*

So the son began walking home. He walked and walked and walked. Soon he saw his father's farm. When he was almost there, he could see someone running down the road toward him! It was his FATHER running to meet him!

"Oh, Father," the son said, "I spent ALL the money you gave me. I am very sorry." The father loved his son and was glad he had come back home. The father gave him new clothes and a ring and other good things. How glad the son was that his father loved him and forgave him.

Jesus told this story to help us learn that God is loving and kind, just like the father in the story. We can show God's love by being kind and forgiving to each other.

Kneeling Man

Collect

Bible, scissors, ruler, white construction paper, poster board, markers, glue or tape.

Prepare

Cut one 9-inch (23-cm) person shape from construction paper for each child. Cut one 6-inch (15-cm) poster-board square for each child.

Do

Children use markers to color and draw facial features on their person shapes. Children bend person shapes at the knees and glue or tape bent legs to poster-board squares to form kneeling men.

Enrichment Ideas

1. Children glue colored tissue squares onto kneeling men to make clothes.

2. Lightly print the words "Thank you" on each poster-board square. Children trace over letters.

One Man Thanks Jesus

Luke 17:11-19

Jesus teaches me to thank God.

Talk About

☺ In today's Bible story, Jesus walked down a road. Some sick men came to Jesus to ask Him for help. Jesus helped them! One man knelt down to thank Jesus for His help. You can make a kneeling man today.

☺ Hannah, I see you are using markers to color your kneeling man. You can thank God for your hands to draw with. What are some other ways you can use your hands?

☺ Jesus teaches us to give thanks to God. We can thank God for the good things He gives us. What are some things you would like to thank God for, Paulina?

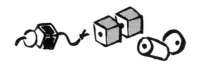

One Man Thanks Jesus

Luke 17:11-19

Our Bible tells us about 10 men who were very sick. They had terrible sore places all over their bodies. They were so sick they couldn't live with their families. They were so sick they couldn't talk with their friends. They were so sick no one would let them come near because no one wanted to catch their disease. Then one day, they heard about Jesus. Jesus walked from town to town telling people about God and helping people. The 10 men heard that Jesus was coming to their town!

The sick men must have talked excitedly. They said, "Maybe Jesus will help us!" They stood far back from the road and watched for Jesus. There He was! The men began to shout, "Jesus! Jesus! Please help us!"

Jesus loves everyone and He loved these sick men. Jesus wanted to make them well. "Go and show the Temple leader that you are now well," He told them.

The 10 men didn't feel well, and they didn't look well. Still, they did what Jesus had told them. As the 10 men walked, suddenly they were made well! They were no longer sick! The sores on their arms and legs were gone. Now they would be able to live with their families and talk with their friends.

One man remembered that it was Jesus who had made them well. He stopped walking. *I must go back and thank Jesus for making me well*, the man must have thought. He began to run back to where Jesus was. He could hardly wait to see Jesus!

When he saw Jesus, he knelt down in front of Jesus and shouted, "Thank You, Jesus, for making me well!"

Paper People Banner

Collect

Bible, white paper, scissors, markers, art materials (yarn, fabric or wallpaper scraps, wiggle eyes, etc.), glue, stapler.

Prepare

Fold white paper and cut out paper dolls (see sketch a), preparing approximately four dolls for each child. On a separate sheet of white paper, print the words "Jesus loves us!"

Do

1. Children use markers and art materials to create facial features and clothing on paper dolls.

2. As children complete dolls, staple doll hands together, forming a paper-doll banner. Staple sheet of paper with "Jesus loves us!" between two of the doll sections (see sketch b). Display banner in classroom or hallway.

Enrichment Ideas

1. Instead of providing precut paper dolls, make paper-doll patterns on poster board, preparing a pattern for each child. Older children trace around patterns on construction paper and cut out paper dolls.

2. Instead of providing a variety of art materials, provide different types of markers (gel, glitter, etc.) to create facial features and clothing on paper dolls.

Jesus Loves Children

Matthew 19:13-15; Mark 10:13-16

Jesus loves and cares for me every day.

Talk About

☼ In today's Bible story, Jesus told His friends to let children come to see Him. Jesus loves and cares for all the children in the world! Let's make a banner of children.

☼ Jayce, I like the happy faces you are drawing. How do you feel when you think about Jesus loving us? Jesus' love makes me feel happy!

☼ Jesus wanted to see the children because He loves all children! Jesus loves and cares for us each day. Jose, what are some good things Jesus helps you have because He loves you?

Jesus Loves Children

Matthew 19:13-15; Mark 10:13-16

One day, some parents had heard that Jesus was coming. They wanted their children to meet Jesus! So they called their children. They probably washed the children's faces. They combed the children's hair. The mothers probably made sure their children were wearing clean clothes. Then off the families went toward the place where Jesus was.

As these families walked closer, they could see that Jesus was busy. He was talking to some grown-ups. But those mothers and fathers wanted their children to meet Jesus! They probably took their children's hands. They went in and out and around the crowd of people. Soon they were close to Jesus. They must have been happy and excited! But just then, some of Jesus' friends stopped the families.

"Stand back!" they said. "Jesus is too busy to see children."

The children and their mothers and fathers felt so sad! They turned to walk away. But wait! They heard Jesus say something.

"Let the children come to Me!" Jesus said. "Do not send the children away. I love children. I want to see them!" Jesus had not wanted His friends to send the children away at all!

Jesus' friends must have felt a little silly. They were surprised that Jesus cared so much about children. Jesus thought that children were just as important as grown-ups.

So the children came to Jesus. Some children probably ran to hug Him. Some children may have stood shyly near Him. A few probably climbed right up onto His lap. Jesus put His arms around them. He prayed for each child. The children must have felt very happy! The children knew that Jesus loved them.

Thankful Books

Collect

Bible, marker, construction paper, magazine or catalog pictures of objects children might share (toys, food, clothing, books, etc.), glue, stapler.

Prepare

For each child, prepare a sheet of paper as shown in sketch a, leaving spaces to print children's names.

Do

Write children's names twice at top of pages. In the open area of their pages, children glue pictures of objects they could share with others. Staple the pages together to make a book and write other children's names once at the bottom of pages (see sketch b). Read completed book aloud to children.

Enrichment Ideas

1. Cut a large sheet of butcher paper. Invite children to glue pictures onto butcher paper to create a mural of things they can share. Display the mural in your classroom.

2. Give each child a sheet of construction paper. Across the top write "Things I can share." Invite children to collect classroom objects. Using markers, children trace around objects on paper. Label each object. Display children's papers.

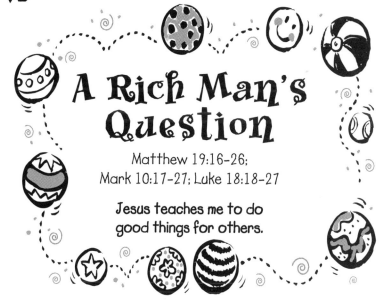

A Rich Man's Question

Matthew 19:16-26;
Mark 10:17-27; Luke 18:18-27

Jesus teaches me to do good things for others.

Talk About

☺ Our Bible story today tells about a man who had lots of money. He probably had lots of clothes to wear, too. Jesus told him to share what he had with poor people. Let's make a book with pictures of things we can share.

☺ Megan, I see you are gluing a picture of a doll on your paper. Sharing dolls with our friends means we take turns playing with the dolls. What is the name of someone in our class you could share with?

☺ Sharing is a way we can show God's love. Who are some people that you can share with at your house, Maureen?

a.
what do you see?
I see sharing with me.

b.
Ryan, Ryan, what do you see?
I see Morgan sharing with me.

Morgan, Morgan, what do you see?
I see Natalie sharing with me.

A Rich Man's Question

Matthew 19:16-26;
Mark 10:17-27; Luke 18:18-27

One day Jesus was walking with His friends. A rich young man ran up to Him. "Teacher, what should I do so that I can live forever?" the young man asked Jesus.

Jesus looked at the man. Jesus said, "You must obey God's rules. Do not kill. Do not take things that do not belong to you. Do not say things that are not true. Show love to your father and mother. Be kind to people."

The rich young man knew these rules. He had learned them when he was a young boy. "Teacher, I have obeyed God's rules since I was a boy," the man said.

Jesus loved this man. Jesus was glad the man had obeyed God's rules. But Jesus knew the man loved his money more than he loved God. So Jesus told him, "You must do one more thing: Sell everything you have. Share the money with others who do not have food and clothes. Then follow Me." Jesus wanted the young man to do good things for others.

The young man's face suddenly became sad. He looked down at the ground. He was very rich. He had lots of money and good things. But he did not want to share. He did not want to do what Jesus said. So the rich young man slowly walked away.

Jesus turned to His friends and said, "It is hard for people who love money to love and obey God."

"You need God's help to love and obey Him," Jesus told His friends. "With God's help, anyone can live with Me forever."

Tree Mural

Collect

Bible, 8-foot (2.4-m) length of butcher paper, markers, tape.

Prepare

On paper, draw a tree with many branches. Cut out a face-shaped hole above a low branch.

Do

1. Children color tree and draw leaves. Tape mural to doorway (see sketch).

2. As one child looks through the hole, lead another child to say, "Zacchaeus! Come down. I want to stay at your house today." Continue until each child has had a turn.

Enrichment Ideas

1. Lead children to use the mural to act out the Bible story.

2. Before class, draw simple leaf shapes on green construction paper. In class, invite children to cut out and glue leaves on butcher paper.

3. Cut brown paper bags into small squares. Show children how to crumple and then smooth out the squares to give pieces the look of tree bark. Invite children to glue pieces onto tree trunk and branches.

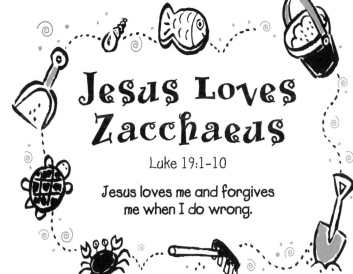

Jesus Loves Zacchaeus

Luke 19:1-10

Jesus loves me and forgives me when I do wrong.

Talk About

☺ In our Bible story today, Zacchaeus was too short to see Jesus, so he climbed up a tree. Zacchaeus had done wrong things. But Jesus wanted to come to his house anyway. Jesus showed that He loved Zacchaeus. Let's make a tree to remind us of this story.

☺ Katie, what if it were your turn to glue leaves on our tree, but someone pushed ahead of you? Would that be a right or a wrong thing to do? What would you do?

☺ When we do wrong things, we can ask Jesus to forgive us. When Jesus forgives us, we know that Jesus loves us. Zoe, what are some wrong things we might need forgiveness for?

Jesus Loves Zacchaeus

Luke 19:1-10

Zacchaeus had a LOT of money. He had a lot of money because he took money that did NOT belong to him! Zacchaeus had done many wrong things by taking this money. People did not like him because of all the times he had taken money that was not his.

One day Jesus came to the town where Zacchaeus lived. *I want to go see Jesus,* he decided. Off he hurried to the road where Jesus was walking. A large crowd of people had come to see Jesus. So when Zacchaeus got there, he couldn't see Jesus! Zacchaeus was very short. Even on tiptoe he could not see over the crowd of people.

But then Zacchaeus had an idea. He ran to a big tree. And he climbed up, up, UP the tree. Now he could see over all the people!

Zacchaeus could see Jesus. Jesus came closer and closer—until Jesus was right under the tree! Jesus stopped and looked up at Zacchaeus.

"Come down, Zacchaeus," said Jesus. "I want to stay at your house today." Zacchaeus climbed down, down, down from that tree. He was surprised that Jesus talked to him! But Zacchaeus was very glad to have Jesus come to his house.

Jesus loves me! Zacchaeus must have thought. He thought about the wrong things he had done. He thought about the money he had wrongly taken away from people. Zacchaeus told Jesus he wanted to give back the money he had taken. And he wanted to give money to the poor people, too! Zacchaeus had learned to love Jesus. Jesus was not angry at him, even though Zacchaeus had done wrong things. Jesus was kind and forgiving to him.

Praise Along the Road

People Praise Jesus

Matthew 21:1-11,15-16; Luke 19:28-38

I can praise Jesus and show my love for Him.

Collect

Bible, 4-foot (1.2-m) length of butcher paper, pencil, green construction paper, scissors, markers, glue, fabric scraps.

Prepare

Outline with pencil a curving road on the butcher paper (see sketch). Make a sample branch.

Do

Children tear or cut green paper to represent palm branches. Children color road, glue fabric scraps and torn or cut green paper to road for coats and palm branches.

Enrichment Ideas

1. Demonstrate how to fringe the edges of paper branches. Children fringe branch shapes before gluing them to mural.

2. Cut coat shapes from construction paper. Children glue fabric scraps to coat shapes and then glue coat shapes to road.

Talk About

☼ In our Bible story, Jesus went to Jerusalem. The people there cut branches from trees and put the branches and their coats on the road. They wanted to show how important Jesus was and to praise Him. Let's make a road and put coats and branches on it.

☼ We can show our love for Jesus by thanking Him for the good things He gives us. Alyssa, what do you want to thank Jesus for?

☼ When we praise Jesus, we can sing and talk about how much we love Him. When are some times we sing about Jesus at church?

People Praise Jesus

Matthew 21:1-11,15-16; Luke 19:28-38

What a happy day it was! Jesus and His friends were going to the Temple in the big city of Jerusalem. On the way, Jesus stopped. He said to His friends, "There is a little donkey in the town. Untie it and bring it to Me."

Jesus' friends did just as He asked them. They found the donkey and brought it back to Jesus. Jesus climbed on the donkey's back and began riding to the big city. Clippety-clop, clippety-clop went the donkey's feet. Jesus' friends walked along the road with Him.

Many other people were walking along the road to Jerusalem, too. There were girls and boys, moms and dads, grandmas and grandpas. They were excited to see Jesus! Some people spread their coats on the road. This showed that they welcomed Jesus as if He were a king. Other people cut branches from palm trees and laid them on the road for Jesus' donkey to walk on. What a happy day it was!

Some people ran ahead to tell others, "Jesus is coming! JESUS is coming!" And even MORE people came to see Jesus. They laughed and sang. They shouted, "Hosanna! Hosanna!" ("Hosanna" means "please save us" and was shouted to praise someone.)

It was a wonderful day in the big city of Jerusalem! The children praised Jesus. The moms and dads praised Jesus. The grandparents praised Jesus. EVERYONE who loved Jesus praised Him by singing happy songs to Him.

Play-Dough Coins

Collect

Bible, play dough, coins or ornately carved buttons.

Do

1. Children play with dough and make flat circles.

2. Children press coins or buttons into dough circles to make coin impressions.

The Poor Woman's Gift

Mark 12:41-44

I can show my love for God.

Enrichment Ideas

1. Provide the ingredients for a no-bake dough recipe. Children measure and mix ingredients to make play dough. To make colored dough, add drops of food coloring and then children mix dough.

2. Provide circle-shaped cookie cutters or empty film canisters and rollers for children to use in their dough play.

Talk About

☼ In today's Bible story, Jesus and His friends went to the Temple. There they saw lots of people who were dropping coins into an offering box. One woman gave all her coins to show love for God. Let's use dough to make some pretend coins.

☼ Michelle, here is some dough for you to use. Thank you for sharing your dough with Melina. Sharing is a way to show your love for God. What are some other things you can share?

☼ Jordan, when we talk to God, we can show our love for Him. What can we say to God?

The Poor Woman's Gift

Mark 12:41-44

One day Jesus was in God's beautiful Temple—the place where people came to worship God. Jesus and His friends were walking to the place in the Temple where people dropped money into the offering boxes.

Clatter! Clink! Clank! The coins made such a loud noise as they fell into the box. The rich people dropped their coins into the offering box at the Temple. These rich people had so much money that they were able to give many coins. They may have hoped people would think they loved God a lot because they gave so much money. Jesus sat nearby. He watched the rich people.

Soon the rich people finished giving their money. Then a poor woman walked quietly to the box. This woman did not have much money. She may not have had enough food. But she loved God very much. She quietly dropped two small coins into the box. The coins hardly made any noise at all. The woman turned and walked away.

Jesus said to His friends, "This poor woman gave more money than all the others."

Jesus' friends must have been surprised! *What was Jesus talking about? The rich people had given much more money than the poor woman.*

Jesus explained, "The rich people did put in more coins, but they only gave some of what they have. They still have plenty of money left over."

Jesus' friends thought about the woman's gift. She really had given more than the rich people. She gave all the money she had because she loved God.

Easter Garden

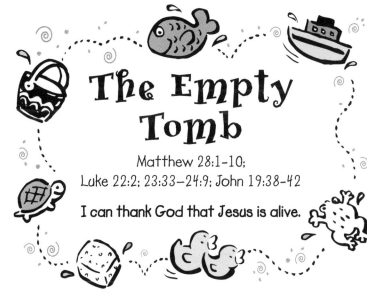

The Empty Tomb

Matthew 28:1-10;
Luke 22:2; 23:33–24:9; John 19:38-42

I can thank God that Jesus is alive.

Collect

Bible, large sheet of butcher paper, crayons or markers, popped popcorn, glue.

Prepare

On butcher paper draw a garden scene with a tomb and several trees (see sketch a).

Do

Children color scene with crayons or markers and glue popcorn to tree branches to make blossoms. Children snack on additional popcorn as they work.

Enrichment Ideas

1. Children make butterflies. Children place small collage items into resealable bags. Assist each child in bending a piece of chenille wire in half. Make sure collage items are evenly distributed. Child gathers bag in center and lays it inside wire. Twist wire around center of bag. Children bend ends of chenille wires to make antennas (see sketch b).

2. Instead of using popcorn, children glue colored cotton balls to trees.

Talk About

☀ In our Bible story today, Jesus' friends went to a garden. They wanted to see the place where Jesus was buried. But Jesus wasn't there. God had made Jesus alive! Jesus' friends were glad to know that Jesus is alive. Let's make a garden to remind us that Jesus is alive!

☀ Jesus' friends were glad that Jesus is alive. How do you think their faces looked? Let's thank God that Jesus is alive!

☀ At Eastertime, we praise and thank God that Jesus is alive. What do we do at Eastertime to show how glad we are that Jesus is alive?

a.

b.

The Empty Tomb

Matthew 28:1-10;
Luke 22:2; 23:33-24:9; John 19:38-42

When Jesus was here on Earth, Jesus did many wonderful things for people. He made blind people see. He helped sick people be well. He taught people about God. Jesus loved people very much. And many people loved Him.

But not everyone loved Jesus. Some people hated Jesus. They wanted to hurt Jesus. They didn't like it that many men and women wanted Jesus to be their leader! These angry people said, "If we let Jesus go on like this, everyone will believe in HIM, and we won't be in charge!" These people hated Jesus so much they killed Him.

Jesus' friends were very sad when Jesus died. They didn't know God's plan for Jesus. The sad friends put Jesus' body in a tomb in a garden. The tomb was a little room cut out of the side of a hill. Jesus' friends rolled a big stone in front of the opening of the tomb.

On the first day of the week, some women who were Jesus' friends walked to the tomb. The women were still very sad. They thought Jesus' body was in the tomb. But when the women got to the tomb, God had a big surprise for them! The big stone in front of the tomb had been moved. Jesus' body was GONE.

Suddenly, the women saw two angels. The angels wore shining white clothes. "Jesus is not dead," the angels said. "He is alive!" NOW Jesus' friends weren't sad anymore. The women were happy and thankful to hear this good news! The women ran to share the glad news with Jesus' other friends. "Jesus IS alive!" they shouted.

Happy Faces

Collect

Bible, white paper, marker, a variety of items that can be used to make dots (dot stickers, bingo marker bottles, stamps and stamp pads, etc.).

Prepare

For each child, draw a large happy face on a sheet of paper.

Do

Children cover lines of happy face with dots.

Enrichment Ideas

1. Print the words "Jesus is alive" on each child's paper.

2. Children wear paint shirts. Give each child a sheet of finger-paint paper. Pour several drops of paint onto paper. Invite children to finger-paint, drawing happy faces on their papers.

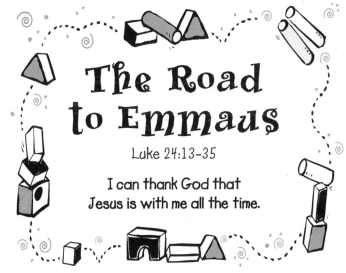

The Road to Emmaus

Luke 24:13-35

I can thank God that Jesus is with me all the time.

Talk About

☀ In today's Bible story, Jesus' friends were glad to know that Jesus is alive. Let's make some happy faces to show that we are happy and thankful Jesus is alive, too!

☀ Miguel, you are making a happy-face picture. Where is a place that you are happy to go? Jesus is with you when you go to the pizza parlor.

☀ Victor, where do you like to go? We can thank God that Jesus is with you when you play at your friend's house. Let's thank God that Jesus is with us.

The Road to Emmaus

Luke 24:13-35

Two of Jesus' friends were very sad. They were sad because Jesus had died. The two friends slowly walked down a road. They were walking from the big city of Jerusalem to the little town of Emmaus (eh-MAA-uhs). As they walked, they talked about Jesus. They talked about the sad day when Jesus died. They wondered about the stories they had heard that Jesus was alive again. *How could Jesus be alive?* They did not know what to think!

As the two walked along, a man came up and walked with them. The man asked them, "What are you talking about?"

"Don't you know what has happened?" one friend asked. "We thought Jesus was our king. But some people who hated Jesus killed Him. Jesus is dead." The friends were sad.

The man continued to walk and talk with them. When they came to the town of Emmaus, it was time to eat. The two friends said to the man, "Stay and eat with us." The man did stay with them. When the dinner was ready, the man picked up some bread and prayed. Then He took pieces of the bread and handed them to the two friends. Right then the two friends knew the man was Jesus! They were so excited! Jesus is alive! But suddenly, Jesus was gone.

Even though it was nighttime, the two friends hurried back to Jerusalem. They found other friends of Jesus. The two friends told the others, "Jesus is alive!" Everyone who heard this good news was very happy and thankful.

Handy Place Mats

Collect

Bible, construction paper, crayons or markers; optional—clear Con-Tact paper.

Do

Help children trace around their hands on construction paper. Children color handprints to make place mats. Children name family members to whom they want to give place mats. (Optional: Cover place mats with clear Con-Tact paper.)

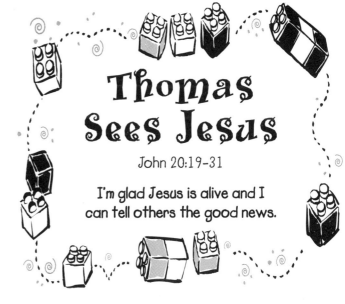

Thomas Sees Jesus

John 20:19-31

I'm glad Jesus is alive and I can tell others the good news.

Enrichment Ideas

1. Children use stamp pads to make fingerprints on place mats.

2. Children make handprints using paint. With a brush, paint a thin layer of paint on children's hands. Children make handprints on paper.

3. Children cut around handprints and glue cutouts onto sheets of different-colored construction paper.

Talk About

☺ In our Bible story today, Jesus showed a man named Thomas that He is really alive. Jesus asked Thomas to touch His hands. Let's trace around our hands.

☺ Pilar, you are coloring your hands red. When Thomas touched Jesus' hands, he knew Jesus is alive. It's good news to know that Jesus is alive.

☺ Thomas was glad Jesus is alive. Riley, who is in your family? You can tell your sister that Jesus is alive.

Thomas Sees Jesus

John 20:19-31

One night some of Jesus' friends were eating together in a house. They were very sad. Their friend Jesus had been killed three days ago. They knew Jesus' body was not in the tomb. They had heard people say they had seen Jesus and that He was alive! But some of them were having a hard time believing that Jesus was really alive. As the friends were talking, Jesus came into the room. Jesus' friends were surprised and a little afraid. How could this be Jesus? He is supposed to be dead!

Jesus must have smiled at them. "Why are you afraid?" Jesus asked. Jesus held out His hands, so His friends could see the hurt places on them. Then Jesus asked for something to eat. When the friends saw Jesus and heard His kind voice, they knew He was really alive. The friends were not afraid anymore. This was REALLY Jesus!

But Jesus' friend named Thomas was not there when Jesus came. Later, Jesus' other friends told Thomas that Jesus was alive, but Thomas shook his head. Thomas told the friends, "I will not believe that Jesus is alive unless I see Him and touch Him."

A week later, all the friends and Thomas were together in the same house again. Suddenly, Jesus came into the room, just as He had done before. Jesus knew that Thomas still didn't believe He was really alive. Jesus must have smiled at Thomas. "Thomas," Jesus said, "look at My hands. Touch them. I want you to know that I am alive."

Thomas loved Jesus. He looked at Jesus and said, "My Lord and my God!" Now Thomas knew for sure that Jesus is alive. And he was very glad.

Let's Go Fishing

Collect

Bible, light blue construction paper, markers, 3x6-inch (7.5x15-cm) brown paper rectangles for boats, glue, 6-inch (15-cm) nylon net fabric squares for fishnets, fish-shaped crackers; optional—craft sticks.

Do

Children draw waves on blue paper and glue boats and one corner of fish nets onto paper. Children glue fish crackers in waves or under nets. (Optional: Children glue craft sticks to boats to make masts.)

Jesus Lives Today

Matthew 28:16-20; Luke 24:50-53; John 21:1 14; Acts 1:3-11

I'm glad Jesus is alive and always with me.

Talk About

☼ In our Bible story today, Jesus came to see His friends while they were fishing. Jesus helped them fill their nets with lots of fish! Jesus' friends were glad Jesus is alive. Jesus promised to always be with them. Let's make fishing pictures to remind us of today's story.

☼ Ethan, where do you like to go? Jesus is with you at your friend's house. I'm glad Jesus is alive and always with us.

☼ Jesus' friends were glad to hear His promise to always be with them. They were glad to know that Jesus is alive. Mackenzie, where do you like to play? Jesus is with you in your backyard.

Enrichment Ideas

1. Children draw stick-figure fishermen on boats.

2. Children glue blue tissue-paper squares to their ocean scenes.

3. Children use watercolors to paint fishing scenes. After paint is dry, children glue fish crackers to their papers.

Jesus Lives Today

Matthew 28:16-20; Luke 24:50-53;
John 21:1-14; Acts 1:3-11

Jesus had died, but now He was alive again. Jesus' friends were so happy that Jesus was alive! Jesus stayed with His friends for many days. Jesus talked with them about many things. He loved His friends! Once when they were fishing, Jesus helped them catch lots of fish. Their nets were so full of fish that the friends could barely lift them up from the water! That same day Jesus cooked some breakfast for His friends. Jesus told them that someday soon He would be going back to heaven.

Then the day came when it was time for Jesus to go back to heaven. He walked with His friends out in the country. Jesus said to His friends, "Remember that I am with you always. I will watch over you and take care of you. Someday I will come back, and we will be together in heaven." Jesus wanted them to know that even though they wouldn't see Jesus with their eyes, He was still with them. Jesus' friends listened quietly. "After I am gone," Jesus said, "go and tell people everywhere that I love them."

Then Jesus rose up off the ground! Jesus' friends must have been surprised! Jesus went up and up and UP, until He was in the clouds, and then His friends couldn't see Him anymore. They stood there, looking up.

Suddenly, there were two angels standing beside the friends. The angels said, "Why are you standing here looking into the sky? Jesus has gone to heaven! Jesus will come back again someday." Jesus' friends were very glad! Now they knew Jesus was going to come back, just as He had promised. And they were glad because Jesus is alive and had promised to always be with them. And He will always be with us, too!

Rubber-Band Man

Collect

Bible, paper, ruler, scissors, crayons, large rubber bands, stapler.

Prepare

For each child, from paper cut one 6x9-inch (15x23-cm) rectangle for a body, two 1x2-inch (2.5x5-cm) rectangles for feet and one 4-inch (10-cm) circle for a face.

Do

Children draw faces on circles, and clothing on rectangle body. Help children assemble figures by stapling faces to body, and rubber-band legs to body and feet.

The Lame Man Walks

Acts 3:1-16

I can obey God by helping others.

Talk About

☼ Today in our Bible story, a man's legs were lame. He couldn't walk or jump at all. One of Jesus' friends helped this man. God made the man's legs well. The man jumped and hopped and thanked God! You can make a man whose legs will hop and jump.

☼ Ashlee, I see you are helping Nathan use the stapler. You are obeying God when you help others. What are some other ways you can help in our classroom?

☼ Jesus' friends obeyed God by helping others. Chloe, who are some people you can help? What things can you do to help them?

Enrichment Ideas

1. Draw rectangle and circle patterns and invite children to trace around them and cut them out.

2. Children glue fabric scraps to men for clothing.

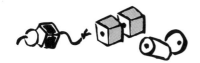

The Lame Man Walks

Acts 3:1-16

Near the gate outside the Temple sat a man who couldn't walk. His legs were lame. That means they didn't work. He couldn't even stand up. Every day this man's friends carried him up the hill to the Temple gate. The Temple was the place where many people went to pray and learn about God. Every day the lame man sat by the Temple. As people walked into the Temple, the man would ask them for money.

One day Jesus' friends Peter and John walked up the hill to the Temple. Peter and John heard someone call, "Please give me some money." They stopped. They looked down. They saw the lame man sitting on the ground.

"I have no money," Peter said, "but I do have something to give you." Peter reached out and took the man's hand. Peter said, "In the name of Jesus, stand up and walk!" and he pulled the man to his feet.

Suddenly, the lame man's feet and legs were strong! The man began to walk! Then the man began to skip and jump and hop and RUN! He was so happy! He went into the Temple with Peter and John. The man told everyone what happened. "Thank You, God! I can walk," said the man.

The people at the Temple saw the man walking. They thought Peter and John had made the man walk. But Peter told them, "We did not make this man walk. Jesus made his legs strong." Peter told all those people about Jesus. And the man who now could walk learned about Jesus, too. Peter and John must have been glad they had obeyed God by helping others.

Sharing Books

Barnabas Shares

Acts 4:32-37

I can help others
by sharing with them.

Collect

Bible, three large index cards for each child, tape, scissors, magazine pictures of items children might share.

Prepare

Fold each index card in half widthwise.

Do

Help each child tape three cards together to make an accordion book. On each page of the book, child glues pictures of things they like to share.

Enrichment Ideas

1. Children "read" their books by pointing at pictures and telling about the things they can share.

2. Give children markers and invite children to write words in their books. (Remember that children's marks are fine. They don't need to write actual words.)

3. Provide children with a variety of stickers. On their pages, children can put stickers of things they want to share.

Talk About

☼ In our Bible story today, Jesus' friends shared food and clothes. We help others by sharing with them. Let's make some books with pictures of things we can share.

☼ Gina, Michael needs some scissors. How can you help? Thank you, Gina, for sharing the scissors. We share by giving things to people who need them.

☼ God wants us to help people in need by sharing with them. Danae, who are some people that you can share with in our classroom? At your home?

Barnabas Shares

Acts 4:32-37

One of the ways Jesus' friends showed their love was by sharing everything they had. Nobody had to ask them to share. They wanted to share!

Some people had lots of food and clothing. But they didn't keep it all for themselves. They shared their food and clothes with Jesus' friends who had no food and clothing. If a family had more food than they needed, they didn't throw it away. They gave it to Jesus' friends who did not have enough food.

One of Jesus' friends helped other people so much that his friends gave him a nickname. The man's friends called him Barnabas. "Barnabas" meant something like "Mr. Helper." He was a cheerful, happy man. Barnabas was always helping people and trying to cheer them up!

Barnabas owned a field. He could have kept it for himself. Instead, Barnabas sold his field. Someone bought the land and gave Barnabas money for it. Barnabas could have spent that money on something he wanted for himself, but he didn't. Barnabas gave the money to the men who loved Jesus. He said, "Here, share this money with people who need it."

Barnabas had learned about Jesus and what Jesus said to do. He knew Jesus wanted him to help other people. Barnabas didn't keep his field or his money for himself. He showed he loved Jesus by sharing with other people.

My Sandwich

Collect

Bible, 4-inch (10-cm) squares of white paper (about five for each child), crayons or markers, tape.

Do

Child draws bread and fillings on paper squares to make sandwiches or hamburgers. (For example, a child might draw two hamburger buns, a hamburger patty and a piece of cheese.) Tape edges of completed sandwich or hamburger together on one side.

Enrichment Ideas

1. Challenge children to think of foods beginning with each letter of the alphabet. If a child gives a silly response, simply smile and comment, **Trevor, it would be pretty silly to eat monsters! What would you really like to eat?**

2. Before class, collect all of the items needed to make real sandwiches. In class, invite children to create their own sandwiches. Post a note alerting parents to the use of food in this activity. Also check registration forms for food allergies.

Food for Widows

Acts 6:1-7

I'm glad to help others by being kind.

Talk About

☼ In our Bible story, Jesus' friends were kind to some women who had no food. They gave the women food and made sure they had enough to eat. Let's make some pretend sandwiches to remind us of today's story.

☼ Thank you for sharing the markers, Denise. You are being kind. What's your favorite sandwich? What goes inside the bread?

☼ When we are kind to others, we help them be happy. And we feel happy, too. What are some ways we can be kind to others in our classroom?

Food for Widows

Acts 6:1-7

Every day Jesus' friends told more and more people the good news that Jesus loved them. More and more people learned to love Jesus. And every day these people were sharing their food and clothing with people who had none. They were very happy.

However, one group of women whose husbands had died were not happy. These women said, "No one is sharing food with us. We are not getting enough to eat!" This was a problem!

The people who were friends of these women could have gotten angry. They could have grumbled and argued and caused lots of trouble, but they didn't. Instead, they told Jesus' friends about the problem.

When Jesus' friends heard about this, they felt sad. They wanted everyone to have enough food to eat. They wanted to be kind to everyone. So these friends of Jesus called everyone together. "We know it isn't fair that some people don't get enough food to eat." The people listened quietly.

"This is what we will do," Jesus' friends said. "Choose seven special helpers. These special helpers will make sure everyone gets enough food." So the people chose one, two, three, four, five, six, seven men to be special helpers. Then Jesus' friends prayed and asked God to help the seven men do their best work.

These special helpers did a good job. Now the women had enough food to eat, just like everyone else. Everyone worked together to be kind and show they loved Jesus.

Decorated Chariots

Collect

Bible, scissors, white construction paper, markers, glue, wheel-shaped pasta.

Prepare

Cut large triangles from white construction paper for chariots (see sketch a).

Do

Invite children to color chariots using markers. Give each child an 8½ x 11-inch (21.5 x 28-cm) sheet of construction paper. Children glue chariots to paper and glue pasta for chariot wheels. Invite children to use markers to draw stick-figure horses in front of chariots.

Enrichment Ideas

1. Children decorate chariots by cutting bits of colored paper. Children glue paper onto chariots to create a mosaic pattern.

2. Provide a large box with sides cut for a chariot (see sketch b). Children decorate box and then sit in it, pretending to ride in a chariot.

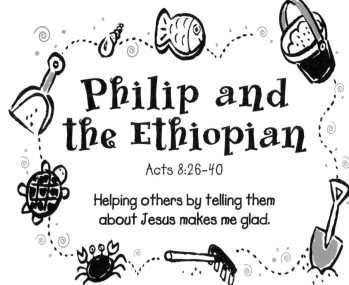

Philip and the Ethiopian

Acts 8:26-40

Helping others by telling them about Jesus makes me glad.

Talk About

☺ In our Bible story, Philip talked to a man riding in a chariot. Philip helped the man learn the good news that Jesus loved him. Let's make chariots to remind us of today's Bible story.

☺ Aretha, you are helping Fred with his wheels. Thank you. Helping others makes us glad. What are some ways you can help your brother at home?

☺ We can help others by telling them the good news about Jesus. Jason, who do you want to tell about Jesus?

a.

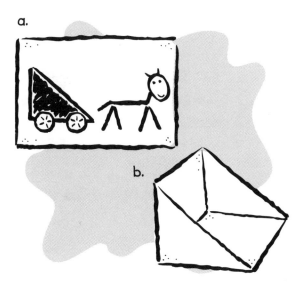

b.

Philip and the Ethiopian

Acts 8:26-40

Philip was one of Jesus' friends. He told many people the good news that Jesus loved them. One day an angel came to see Philip. (Angels are God's special helpers.) This angel told Philip an important message. "There is a road that goes into the desert," the angel said. "God wants you to go walk on that road." Then the angel left.

Philip did exactly what the angel told him. On the road Philip saw some horses running toward him. Philip saw that the horses were pulling a chariot. (A chariot is a small open cart pulled by horses.)

Riding in that chariot was a man from a country in Africa. The man was reading some words from the Bible. The words were written on a scroll. (A scroll is like a long rolled-up sheet of paper.) Philip ran up to the chariot. The man must have looked confused. "Do you understand what you are reading?" Philip asked the man.

"No, I don't. I need someone to tell me what the words mean," the man said. Then the man asked, "Will you talk with me about these words?" So Philip got into the chariot. Together he and the man read the Bible scroll. Philip told the man the good news about Jesus. "God sent Jesus to Earth," Philip might have said. "Jesus is God's Son! Jesus loves you."

The man was happy to hear the good news that Jesus loved him. The man believed that Jesus is God's Son. The man said, "Look! Here is some water. I want to be baptized." (People are baptized to show that they believe in Jesus.) Philip was glad he could help the man learn about Jesus. Then Philip left the man and went to tell other people that Jesus loved them, too.

A Light on the Road

Collect

Bible, sandpaper, scissors, ruler, thick yellow yarn, 9x12-inch (23x30.5-cm) light-blue construction paper, glue, markers.

Prepare

Cut sandpaper into 2-inch (5-cm) squares. For each child, cut four or five lengths of yarn.

Do

As you talk about the Bible story, children glue sandpaper squares onto paper to make road and glue yarn for rays of bright light. Children draw grass, trees, etc. to complete the scene.

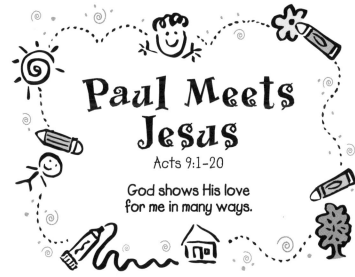

Paul Meets Jesus

Acts 9:1-20

God shows His love for me in many ways.

Enrichment Ideas

1. Children draw stick-figure people walking on road.

2. Instead of sandpaper, children may spread glue on papers and sprinkle sand on glue to make roads.

3. Children use construction paper to draw and then cut out trees, grass, clouds, birds, etc. Children glue cutouts onto road scene.

Talk About

☼ Today in our Bible story, a man named Paul was traveling on a road. Suddenly, Paul saw a bright light and heard the voice of Jesus. Then Paul believed that Jesus is God's Son. We are going to make drawings of a road and bright lights to help us remember the story of Paul.

☼ God loves me and gives me friends. Devon, what friends has God given you to show His love for you?

☼ One way God shows love to us is by giving us good food to eat. Nathan, what kind of fruit do you like to eat? Because God loves us, He makes strawberries to grow.

Paul Meets Jesus

Acts 9:1-20

The Bible tells us that many people loved Jesus. But one man named Paul did NOT love Jesus. Paul was angry so many people loved Jesus! Paul heard that many of the people who loved Jesus lived in a far-away city. "I will go to that city," Paul said. "I'll stop them from talking about Jesus. When I find people who love Jesus, I'll put them in jail!" So Paul and his friends traveled to the city.

On the road near the city, Paul saw a very bright light. Paul was so surprised! He fell to the ground. The light was so bright Paul could not see ANYTHING! Then Paul heard a voice! "Paul, why are you hurting Me?" the voice asked.

"Who are You, Lord?" Paul asked.

The voice said, "I am Jesus, the One you are hurting." Paul must have been surprised! Then Jesus told Paul to go to the city. With his friends' help, Paul did what Jesus said. For three days in the city, he didn't eat or drink anything. Paul still couldn't see, but he prayed to God. While Paul was praying, Jesus spoke to another man in the city. The man's name was Ananias. "Ananias, go to Paul and pray for him," Jesus said.

Ananias was afraid of Paul, but he trusted God. So Ananias obeyed and went to Paul. Ananias prayed for Paul and suddenly, Paul could see again! Now Paul loved Jesus and wanted to obey Him. Paul told others about God's love and that Jesus is God's Son.

Basket on a Wall

Collect

Bible, construction paper, scissors, poster board, hole punch, rope material (yarn, string or twine), measuring stick, markers, transparent tape.

Prepare

Cut one 4-inch (10-cm) construction-paper basket shape for each child. Cut poster-board sheets in half widthwise. Use hole punch to make holes near the top and bottom of poster board, one half sheet for each child. Cut one 21-inch (53.5-cm) length of rope material for each child.

Do

1. Children draw lines on poster board to make stones of the wall. Help children thread rope material through holes, knotting in back to make a loop. Children decorate baskets with markers.

2. Pull knot in yarn to the bottom hole in the back. Help children tape basket to the top of the rope in front (this will allow basket to move all the way up and down the wall).

Enrichment Ideas

1. Provide construction paper circles. Children draw face on one circle and tape it to their basket to show a person riding in the basket.

2. Before class, cut squares from sandpaper. In class, children glue sandpaper squares to make stones of wall.

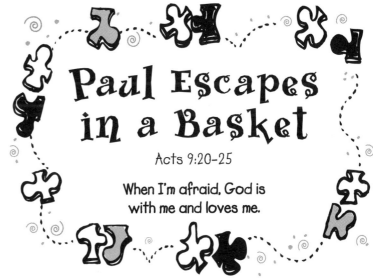

Paul Escapes in a Basket

Acts 9:20-25

When I'm afraid, God is with me and loves me.

Talk About

☼ In our Bible story today, Paul's friends helped him by lowering him over a wall in a basket. Let's make walls with baskets like Paul's.

☼ How do you think Paul felt when angry men wanted to hurt him? Even in this scary time, God was with Paul and loved him.

☼ One way God shows love to us when we're afraid is by giving us people who help us and care for us. Katrina, who helps and cares for you?

Paul Escapes in a Basket

Acts 9:20-25

After Paul met Jesus, he didn't want to hurt the people in God's family anymore. He wanted to tell everyone that Jesus is God's Son. The people in the city where Paul was staying were very surprised that Paul was now one of Jesus' friends. The leaders who sent Paul to hurt Jesus' friends were surprised, too. And they were angry! They decided, "We must stop Paul!"

The leaders sent men to watch the gates of the city. They knew Paul would have to come out of the city gates. They told the men to catch Paul and hurt him. But Paul found out about the leaders' plan. Paul knew he could not leave the city by walking out in the usual way. And of course, God loved Paul and helped him.

One night, some of Paul's new friends met him on the wall of the city. The wall was very high and wide. Paul's friends brought a very big basket and a long, long rope.

Paul climbed into the basket. His friends tied ropes tightly around the basket; and they tied a long, long rope to the basket. Paul's friends held tightly to the rope and slowly pushed the basket over the wall. The basket began to drop down, down, down. Soon there was a THUMP! The basket was on the ground outside the city wall.

Paul was GLAD to climb out of that basket and glad to be out of the city! Paul was glad God loved him and was with him.

Color-and-Sew Robes

Collect

Bible, lightweight poster board, markers, scissors, hole punch, yarn, transparent tape.

Prepare

On poster board, draw robe as shown in sketch. Cut out and use as a pattern to trace one robe on poster board for each child. Cut out robes. Punch holes around edges of robes.

For each robe, cut a piece of yarn twice the circumference of the robe. Knot one end of each piece of yarn to a hole in the robe. Wrap tape around other end of yarn to use as a needle.

Do

Children color the robe with markers. Then each child sews the yarn through the holes in the robe, sewing up and down through the holes or around the outside edges of the poster board.

Enrichment Ideas

1. Children cut out robes and use hole punch to punch holes around the robes' edges.

2. Instead of sewing cards, children glue lengths of different colored yarn to robes to make colorful striped robes.

Peter Helps Dorcas

Acts 9:32-43

I am glad God loves me and helps me.

Talk About

☺ In our Bible story today, Dorcas helped poor people by sewing clothes for them. Let's color and sew robes.

☺ Kaylee, who helps you get dressed in the morning? God helps us by giving us moms and dads who buy clothes and help us get dressed.

☺ I'm glad that God loves us and always helps us. LeeAnn, what did you eat for breakfast? God helps us have good food.

Peter Helps Dorcas

Acts 9:32-43

Dorcas was a very kind woman. Dorcas loved Jesus. She worked hard to help people. One way she helped was by sewing clothes for people who needed them. Dorcas didn't just help people once in a while or whenever she felt like it. Dorcas helped people all the time. And the people Dorcas helped loved her very much.

But one day Dorcas became very sick. She got so sick that she died. Dorcas' friends were very sad. "Maybe Peter can help us," one of them said. Peter was one of Jesus' friends.

"You're right," another may have said. "Let's ask Peter to come here!"

So right away, two men went to get Peter. They hurried to where Peter was. "Peter! Come quickly!" they said. Peter hurried to Dorcas's house with them. The men told Peter what had happened.

Peter went to the room where Dorcas's body had been placed. There were many friends in the room. They were crying. They were sad because their kind friend was dead. The friends showed Peter the clothes Dorcas had made for them. Peter saw how much the friends loved Dorcas. Peter kindly said, "Please leave the room now."

Peter prayed to God. After he prayed, he said, "Dorcas, get up!" And Dorcas opened her eyes and got up! God answered Peter's prayer by making Dorcas alive again! Then Peter called to her friends, and they came and saw Dorcas.

Dorcas was ALIVE! She'd been dead, but now, there she was—standing and smiling at them! Dorcas's friends were so happy that God had helped them by making Dorcas alive again!

Town Mural

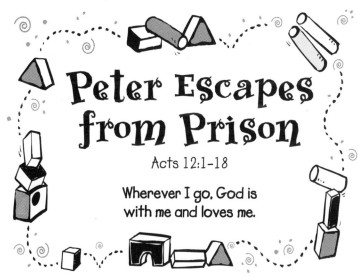

Peter Escapes from Prison

Acts 12:1-18

Wherever I go, God is with me and loves me.

Collect

Bible, large sheet of butcher paper, markers, masking tape, construction paper, scissors, glue.

Prepare

On butcher paper, draw several roads and intersections (see sketch). Tape the butcher paper to table. Cut construction paper into several geometric shapes (squares, rectangles, triangles, etc.).

Do

Children glue construction-paper shapes onto butcher paper to form houses and other buildings. Using markers, children add trees, people, cars and other decorations to mural.

Enrichment Ideas

1. Ask children to name buildings they make (Tom's house, grocery store, restaurant, etc.). Print the names children tell you on index cards. Children tape name cards to their buildings.

2. Provide toy people for children to use in playing with completed mural.

Talk About

☼ In today's Bible story, Peter was put in prison for telling people about Jesus. God sent an angel to help him. Peter walked right out of prison, through the town and over to the house where his friends were praying. God was with Peter. God is with us wherever we go, too! Let's make a picture of some of the places we go.

☼ Bonnie, I see that you are drawing a house. Whose house is it? What are some places you like to go to? God is with you there.

☼ Rusty, where does your mom take you to buy your food? God is with you when you go to the store. God is with you wherever you go!

Peter Escapes from Prison

Acts 12:1-18

Every day more and more people believed that Jesus is God's Son. But some leaders wanted to stop Jesus' friends from telling others about Jesus. They even put some of Jesus' friends in prison!

One day Jesus' friend Peter was put in prison. Peter's friends began to pray to God for help. Peter had chains around him. But that couldn't stop God! One night God sent an angel to Peter.

"Quick, get up!" the angel said. Peter looked down. The chains around him fell off his hands! Peter got dressed and followed the angel. The guards were all asleep. The gates to the prison opened. Peter and the angel walked outside into the street.

Peter thought he was dreaming. Then the angel was gone! Peter knew that God had rescued him from the prison! Peter walked right to the house where he knew his friends were praying for God's help. Peter couldn't wait to tell them what God had done! He knocked at the door. A servant girl named Rhoda came to answer the knock. Before she answered the door, she asked, "Who is it?"

"It's me!" said Peter.

Rhoda knew that voice! She was so excited she forgot to answer the door! She ran back to tell the people who were praying. "PETER is at the door!" she shouted.

Everyone looked up at her in surprise. "You're wrong," some of them said.

"No!" she said. "It's really Peter!" All this time Peter was still knocking at the door! Finally his friends opened the door. Peter's friends were amazed. God had been with Peter, even in prison. And God had answered their prayers!

Baggie Hearts

Collect

Bible, one resealable plastic bag for each child, permanent marker, finger paint or ketchup.

Prepare

Use permanent marker to draw a heart shape on the outside of each bag, and put a small amount of finger paint or ketchup in each bag.

Do

Children lay bags on a flat surface and use their fingers to trace over heart shape.

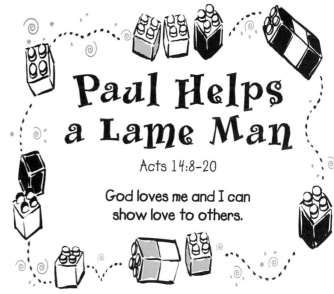

Paul Helps a Lame Man

Acts 14:8-20

God loves me and I can show love to others.

Talk About

☼ In our Bible story today, God made a lame man's legs well. God helped the man because God loved him. God loves us, too! Let's trace heart shapes to remind us of God's love.

☼ Thank you, Todd, for making room for Andrea to sit at the table. You showed God's love by being kind to her! What other kind things can you do at the art table?

☼ God loves us! And God wants us to show His love to others. Gina, what are some ways you help your mom at the store? When we help others, we show love to them.

Enrichment Ideas

1. Children may trace the letter J for the word "Jesus" or trace their own initials.

2. Cut large heart shapes from finger-paint paper. Pour a small amount of paint (use a variety of colors) onto paper. Invite children to use their hands to paint, making hearts on the paper.

Paul Helps a Lame Man

Acts 14:8-20

Paul and his friend Barnabas traveled together. They walked from town to town. In every town, they told people about Jesus. Paul and Barnabas helped people who were sick. Many, many people believed that Jesus is God's Son because of Paul and Barnabas.

One day, Paul and Barnabas came to a town called Lystra. They told the people there that Jesus is God's Son. They told how Jesus healed people. Paul and Barnabas told the people that God loved them. As Paul talked, he looked at one man in the crowd. This man had never walked in his whole life. His feet didn't work. The man looked back at Paul. Paul could see that the man believed God could make his feet well!

So Paul said to the man, "Stand up on your feet!" The man jumped up on his feet. He began to walk. The man may have tried to hop a little and then maybe to run a little. He must have been so happy to use his feet that maybe he twirled a little! His feet were well! God had made the man's feet work!

The people in the crowd saw the man leaping and jumping! The people got VERY excited! They thought Paul and Barnabas had healed the man! But Paul and Barnabas didn't heal the man. Paul and Barnabas told everyone that God had made the man's feet work.

Paul said, "We are here to bring the good news about God." Then Paul and Barnabas walked to other cities to tell others about God. They wanted to show God's love to everyone!

Purple Collages

Collect

Bible, purple collage materials (scrap paper, yarn, fabric scraps, etc.), glue sticks, white construction paper, markers.

Do

1. Children glue collage materials onto white construction paper.

2. After the glue has dried, children may wish to use markers to outline the collage shapes and add other designs.

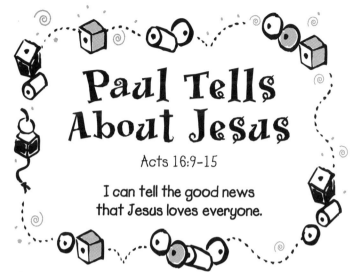

Paul Tells About Jesus

Acts 16:9-15

I can tell the good news that Jesus loves everyone.

Talk About

☀ Our Bible story is about a woman named Lydia. Lydia made money by selling purple cloth. Paul told Lydia the good news about Jesus. Paul told Lydia that Jesus loved her. Let's make purple collages to remind us of Lydia.

☀ Lauren, I see you sharing your purple tissue paper with Dylan. Thank you. Sharing is a way to show Jesus' love. Jesus loves everyone. Who can you tell about God's love?

☀ Paul told Lydia the good news about Jesus. Andy, who can you tell the good news that Jesus loves everyone?

Enrichment Ideas

1. Provide purple play dough for children to play with.

2. Before class, cut several Bible-times coat patterns from poster board. In class, invite interested children to trace around coat patterns onto white construction paper. Give each child a paintbrush and purple paint to paint coats.

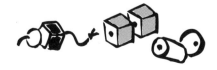

Paul Tells About Jesus

Acts 16:9-15

Paul was a man who loved God very much. Paul wanted everyone to know about Jesus, God's Son. Up and down the dusty roads Paul would walk. He would stop in towns and tell the good news: "God loves you and Jesus is His Son."

One night, Paul had a dream. In the dream, a man asked him to please come to his country. After Paul woke up, he and his friends got into a boat. They sailed to a big town in that country.

The big town was called Philippi. It was near the ocean. Many people came there to buy and sell things. One thing people bought and sold there was cloth dyed a beautiful purple color.

Paul and his friends walked alongside a river. They found a group of women. The women had come together to pray. These women loved God. They wanted to hear all about Jesus and His love. Paul told them about Jesus. Paul's words were good news!

Many women believed Paul's words. One woman who believed in Jesus was named Lydia. Lydia sold purple cloth. She probably sold the cloth to rich people. She probably had a big house. Lydia was baptized. So was everyone in her house. They all showed they believed in Jesus.

Now Lydia was part of God's family, so she wanted to share! Lydia asked Paul and his friends to stay at her house. She wanted to help them. Paul and his friends stayed at Lydia's house. Paul and his friends had come a long, long way to tell people in Philippi the good news of Jesus' love!

Musical Fun

Collect

Bible, a plastic lid or small paper plate and four 16-inch (40.5-cm) lengths of curling ribbon for each child, tape; optional—stickers, children's music cassette/CD and player.

Do

Children tape ribbons onto lids or paper plates. (Optional: Children place stickers onto lids or plates.) Sing songs as children tap lids with hands or wave lids in the air. (Optional: Play music on cassette/CD.)

Singing in Jail

Acts 16:16-34

I can sing songs that tell about Jesus.

Enrichment Ideas

1. Lead children in waving streamers in figure-eight patterns, to the side, over head, etc.

2. Provide paper plates, cups, tape, collage materials, etc. for children to create their own instruments. Have beans or other fillers available for those who want to create instruments that make noise when shaken.

Talk About

☼ In our Bible story, two men, Paul and Silas, were put in jail, even though they had not done anything wrong. Paul and Silas sang songs about Jesus. Other people heard about Jesus because of the songs they sang. Let's make some instruments and sing songs, too.

☼ Hailey, when have you heard someone tell or sing about Jesus? We're glad to sing about Jesus and His love for us.

☼ Wherever Paul and Silas went, they told others about Jesus. Christopher, where can you tell others about Jesus? We can sing songs and tell others about Jesus wherever we are!

Singing in Jail

Acts 16:16-34

Paul and his friends traveled to different places to tell people about Jesus. One day Paul and his friend Silas went to the city of Philippi. They told people about Jesus. But some of the people in Philippi did not like hearing about Jesus. These men were angry! These men took Paul and Silas to the leaders of the city. The men told lies about Paul and Silas. Even though Paul and Silas had done nothing wrong, they were put in jail! The jailer put their feet in pieces of wood called stocks. Paul and Silas could hardly even move!

Paul and Silas probably hurt all over! But they didn't get mad at the jailer or the angry people. They knew God cared about them. So they prayed! They thanked God. Then Paul and Silas sang! They praised God. All the other people in jail could hear them!

Suddenly the ground began to shake, harder and harder. It was an EARTHQUAKE! The doors to the jail broke open! The jailer was afraid all the prisoners would run away. He was sure that he would be in big trouble.

But Paul called out, "Don't worry! We are all here!" The jailer ran to Paul and Silas. He asked, "What must I do to be saved?" Paul and Silas said, "Believe in Jesus!" The jailer and his whole family listened to the good news about Jesus. They believed in Jesus! The family took care of Paul and Silas. They ate a big meal together!

In the morning, the leaders told Paul and Silas they were free to leave. Paul and Silas started walking to a new town. It was time to tell other people about Jesus! Paul and Silas told about Jesus by talking. They told about Jesus by praying. They told about Jesus by singing! Many people heard God's good news about Jesus.

Who's in the Crowd?

Collect

Bible, glue sticks, a variety of pictures of people cut from catalogs or magazines, construction paper.

Do

1. Children glue people pictures to construction paper to make a large crowd scene. Talk with children about the people who listened to Paul in the Bible story.

2. Play a game like I Spy with children. **I spy someone in our crowd with black hair and a red dress.** Children identify person. Continue game as time and interest permit.

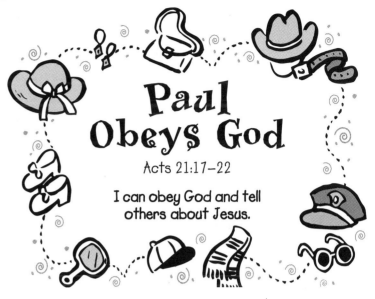

Paul Obeys God

Acts 21:17—22

I can obey God and tell others about Jesus.

Talk About

☀ In our Bible story today, Paul obeyed God and told a big crowd of people about Jesus. Many people listened to Paul. Let's make some pictures of a crowd of people.

☀ Robert, how many people do you want to glue to our picture? We can glue many people to our picture to make a crowd.

☀ Cody, who is someone in your family you can tell that Jesus is God's Son? I'm glad we can obey God and tell others about Jesus.

Enrichment Ideas

1. Children glue people pictures to craft sticks to make puppets.

2. Tape a large sheet of butcher paper to a table. Draw a variety of circles in different colors and sizes. Children draw faces in circles to represent a large crowd. Some children may wish to add stick-figure bodies to faces.

Paul Obeys God

Acts 21:17–22

Everywhere Paul went he told people about Jesus. One day Paul went to the Temple. Some people were angry because Paul told about Jesus. These angry people saw Paul in the Temple. "Look!" they shouted. "This is the man we don't like!"

The angry people grabbed Paul and dragged him out of the Temple. Some soldiers heard the noise and ran to see what was happening.

The leader of the soldiers thought Paul had done something wrong. He put chains on Paul's hands and feet. "Who is this man? What did he do?" the leader asked.

Everyone started shouting at the same time. The army leader couldn't understand what the people were saying. The army leader told the soldiers to take Paul away from the crowd.

The angry, noisy crowd followed Paul and the soldiers. Paul asked, "May I talk to the people?" The leader told Paul he could talk. The crowd became quiet. Paul said, "I used to hurt people who loved Jesus. But now I don't. God has told me to tell all people the good news that Jesus is God's Son. And I am obeying God."

Even though the people were angry at Paul, Paul obeyed God. Paul obeyed God by telling that Jesus is God's Son.

Whistling Wind

Collect

Bible, paper plates, scissors, crepe-paper streamers, ruler, markers, glue.

Prepare

For each child, in the center of a paper plate, cut a hole approximately ½ inch (1.3 cm) in diameter. For each child, cut two or three crepe-paper strips, each approximately ½ inch (1.3 cm) wide and 6 to 8 inches (15 to 20.5 cm) long.

Do

1. Children use markers to draw clouds and skies on paper plates. Assist children as they glue crepe-paper strips above the hole in paper plate. (Note: Make sure hole is not blocked by glued strips.)

2. Holding plates up to their face, children blow through hole to make crepe-paper strips move.

Enrichment Ideas

1. Attach crepe-paper strips before class. Children glue cotton balls to paper plates to make clouds and blow through hole to make streamers move.

2. Children glue lengths of tinsel or silver ribbon to bottom edge of paper plate to represent rain.

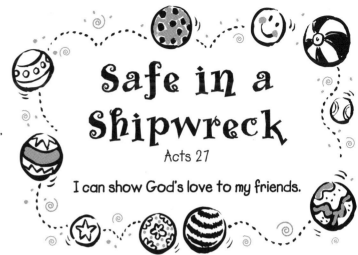

Safe in a Shipwreck

Acts 27

I can show God's love to my friends.

Talk About

☼ In today's Bible story, a strong wind blew Paul's boat out to sea. Then a big storm sent rain down on the boat. The people on the boat were scared. Paul showed God's love to the people by helping them. Let's make something we can blow through to remind us of this story.

☼ Trevor, Lisa needs to use the glue. How can you help her? Thank you for handing her the glue! Helping our friends is a way to show God's love to them.

☼ Lizzie, who are some of your friends? What can you do to show God's love to them?

Safe in a Shipwreck

Acts 27

Paul and many other people climbed onto a big boat. They were going on a long trip across a big sea of water.

While they were on the boat, the wind began to blow. It blew the boat out on the sea. For many days and nights the boat sailed.

Then the wind began to blow harder and harder. The waves splashed higher and higher. The waves rocked the boat up and down and from side to side. Splash! Splash! The waves splashed high in the air and into the boat. The waves almost knocked the boat over! Big dark clouds covered the sky. Rain came pouring down. It was very dark. No one could see the stars at night or the sun during the day. Everyone on the boat was afraid. They thought they were going to drown!

Paul cared for the people on the boat. He told them good news. "Don't be afraid," Paul said. "No one will be hurt." The people wondered why Paul said this.

"God sent an angel to tell me God will take care of all of us. He will keep us all alive. I know that God will do what He says He is going to do." Paul trusted God. He knew that God would care for them.

Early one morning, the people saw land! They tried to sail to the shore. But the big strong waves pushed the boat into some sand just under the water. Crash! The boat began to break apart. All the people jumped into the water. Some people started swimming. Other people grabbed pieces of the broken boat and floated. They found their way to the land. Every person was safe! The people who had been on the boat were glad Paul was a good friend and showed God's love to them. And everyone was thankful God had kept them safe.

Bible Story Character Index